THE EDGE

THE EDGE

Is the Military Dominance of
the West Coming to an End?

Mark Urban

Little, Brown

LITTLE, BROWN

First published in Great Britain in 2015 by Little, Brown

1 3 5 7 9 10 8 6 4 2

A CIP catalogue record for this book
is available from the British Library.

ISBN 978-1-4087-0583-4

Typeset in Bembo by M Rules
Printed and bound in Great Britain by
Clays Ltd, St Ives plc

Papers used by Little, Brown are from well-managed forests
and other responsible sources.

Little, Brown
An imprint of
Little, Brown Book Group
100 Victoria Embankment
London EC4Y 0DY

An Hachette UK Company
www.hachette.co.uk

www.littlebrown.co.uk

For Emanuel and Carmel

Contents

Introduction

In December 2014, at a Whitehall Christmas party, I found myself in conversation with a senior officer in the Royal Navy. We were discussing the multiple threats to national security that had emerged during the previous months – in Ukraine and the Middle East – and how the British government, despite these, appeared to be contemplating further defence cuts. 'We need a Churchill,' he said, looking into the middle distance, 'but I don't see any signs of one emerging.'

Today, then, there are people high up in the government who believe the Western world is facing a situation comparable to that of the 1930s. Indeed, quite a few politicians from Nato and Nordic countries explicitly compared the actions of the Russian President Vladimir Putin in Ukraine to those of Adolf Hitler. Personally, I find this parallel unacceptably simplistic, and can see why it's also very offensive to Russians. And if the situation really is as serious as what happened back then, why are so many Western leaders continuing to reduce their defences rather than launching the type of full-scale rearmament drive that the senior naval officer I spoke to at Christmas was longing for?

Whatever the exact significance of the Ukraine crisis, some very serious changes are taking place in the international system, and it is the purpose of this short book to alert readers to the importance of this historical moment. Western countries, beset by economic woes, are continuing the post-Cold War process of disarmament at the very moment that many would say a new Cold War is starting, and, more widely, the balance of global power is tilting markedly away from them.

There is a tangible sense of foreboding among many senior Western officials. Oddly, this concern about the broad trend of developments is being overlooked by much media reporting because of a preoccupation with the daily detail of the news agenda. But I have been hearing these views from a broad range of government practitioners for some time now. Some, like the naval man above, will not be named because they are still serving, but throughout this text you will find quotes from people who have until recently held top positions in the military, as well as some other thinkers and academics. They have agreed to my quoting our recent correspondence or conversations, even though some would usually be characterised as 'media shy'. They are all, however, alive to the dangers of this moment.

While the Western will to shape the world, as well as its capability to do so, ebbs away, growing nationalism is hampering international cooperation and fuelling conflict, while meanwhile newly empowered non-state groups (and indeed some governments) are tearing up many of the conventions of acceptable international behaviour. That, then, is my purpose: to show how rapidly the global balance of power is shifting away from the West, and to examine some of the implications.

1

The Tides of Power

The Spithead Naval Review of June 1977 was one of those ceremonial occasions at which Britain excels. Scores of warships anchored in the Solent, pennants flying and sailors cheering as the Queen cruised by in the Royal Yacht. Dozens of naval helicopters performed a fly-past, and those unable to attend the spectacle were treated to a full-scale BBC outside broadcast.

The fleet lying at anchor was much smaller than that of the Coronation Review of the Fleet in 1953, and that of today hardly resembles the Royal Navy of

1977. Spithead, though, was a snapshot of British naval power as it drained away on an ebb-tide every bit as powerful and irresistible as those Solent currents feared by weekend dinghy sailors.

As a sixteen-year-old anxious to see the spectacle, but without the Royal Yacht at my disposal, I reviewed the fleet two days before the Queen, from an Isle of Wight ferry. I had gone there to see the aircraft carrier HMS *Ark Royal*, rows of frigates with such names as *Naiad*, *Euryalus* and *Ariadne*, that evoked not just Nelson's victories but also the classical era, and to see the sinister shark-like profiles of *Oberon*-class submarines like *Ocelot* and *Osiris*. I was spellbound at the scale of it.

Today, Britain has no operating aircraft carrier, though it plans to get back into that business soon, and it has no diesel submarines like the O-class at all. Meanwhile its force of destroyers and frigates, the workhorses of the surface fleet, has shrunk from seventy at the time of Spithead to nineteen today.

This story of disappearing naval power could just as easily be applied to the other armed services. A couple of years after Spithead, I signed up as a 'gap year' officer in the Royal Tank Regiment. For a short, heady time I was the commander of one of the British Army's nine hundred Chieftain tanks. Now there are fewer than two hundred tanks in service.

Britain's post-war stepping back from global power was marked by a series of defence reviews – or cuts, in layman's terms – in 1957, 1974 and 1981. Undoubtedly, though, the end of the Cold War gave the greatest impetus to this process, at least in my lifetime. The 1990 package of cuts, called Options for Change, came in the year after the fall of the Berlin Wall, and presented Britain with its long-awaited peace dividend.

The 'Soviet threat', the driver for decades of defence spending, had collapsed and there could be no justification for the continued diversion of resources from the civilian economy. Like many other veterans of the Cold War, I embraced this wholeheartedly and was quite unsentimental about the disbandment or amalgamation of many regiments, including the one in which I had served. Such ebbs and flows in the status of great powers are familiar enough to students of history. While I might love reading about Nelson's or Wellington's victories, the harsh realities of ships paid off or officers put on half pay at the end of the Napoleonic Wars were an integral part of Britain's national story. A child of the 1960s, I had absolutely no hankering after empire.

There was a post-1990 demobilisation across Europe. France, always primarily a land power, took steps that would lead to its army shrinking from 548,000 to the current planned 213,000. The story was the same, whether for a national political elite labouring under the sense that preserving military power was part of preserving their 'top table' status as permanent members of the United Nations Security Council, or for a country in which a completely different history produced equally different attitudes to military power and its use.

So Germany has also wielded the axe, bringing down the *Bundeswehr* from 545,000 soldiers and five thousand tanks to 180,000 and 250 respectively. And countries like Sweden, which as a neutral throughout the Cold War actually maintained one of the highest defence per capita budgets in Europe, slashed their forces mercilessly.

As these organisations shrank, there were a number of consequences. One was that the forces each

European country could deploy fell by a considerably greater margin than the remaining manpower might suggest. In each country the need to maintain a defence ministry, separate service HQs, training schools and all the rest meant keeping proportionately more people in non-combat roles.

Another consequence of the post-Cold War cuts was that many countries gave up entire roles or capabilities. This meant, for example, getting rid of anti-aircraft artillery in one country or submarines in another. The recognition that a nation was not likely to go to war on its own again, and therefore require the full set of capabilities, was in some ways a smart policy that could do something to mitigate that falling ratio of combat to non-combat personal, since taking an entire type of weapon out of service usually carries big savings in terms of training and maintenance. Some reached for the golf-bag analogy in justifying such change, arguing that a full set of clubs was no longer affordable for small or medium-sized European countries. Of course, that's all very well until a country finds itself metaphorically in the bunker with only a putter and a driving iron at its disposal.

While the 9/11 attacks produced a short pause in the downward trend, it had resumed with a vengeance by 2009, as a response to the global financial crisis. Although the US and UK in particular spent colossal sums on their campaigns in Iraq and Afghanistan, this was largely financed by contingency funds and did little to reverse the long-term decline in defence spending. Across Europe, the further cuts to military spending in the five years since the financial crisis have been assessed at 20 to 25 per cent.

The trend continued despite signs – for example the growing turmoil in the Middle East – that international security was deteriorating. From 2012 to 2014, thirteen of the twenty fastest-declining defence budgets could be found in Europe, a cut equivalent to $93 billion being diverted from Europe's military coffers in just two years.

Throughout the last decade, those who believe that there is still room for further defence cuts have looked at the forces that remain and pointed out that Nato, as an alliance, still spends more on defence than the rest of the world put together. But this too is changing.

Behind the bald statistics of Nato's major defence

spending and millions under arms are certain realities that have long been understood by its decision-makers. The positions of the United States and its European allies are fundamentally different. In 2014, only four countries in the alliance met its target of devoting 2 per cent of their economy (or gross domestic product) to defence – and three of them are the UK, Greece and Estonia. It is the other, the American giant, that completely distorts the picture.

However, the assumption that American taxpayers will subsidise everybody else's security, footing three-quarters of the Nato bill, is no longer valid. While a couple of years ago the United States was spending 4.6 per cent of its GDP on the military, that has fallen to 3.9 per cent at the time of writing and the Obama administration has been trying to reduce that to 2.9 per cent by 2017. Along with this shrinking of the defence dollar (at least relative to the size of the wider economy) will come the inevitable further reduction in forces, for example a cut of one quarter in the number of brigades the army can deploy.

In truth, when it comes to its major weapons the US armed forces have, at least since the 1991 Desert

Storm campaign against Iraq, been living off the investment made in the late Cold War years by the Reagan administration. Many of the systems bought then, from M1 tanks to F-16 fighters and *Los Angeles*-class submarines have been soldiering on ever since (albeit with upgrades), leading to an ageing stock of weapons. And it's not as if the Pentagon has been immune to post-Cold War cuts either.

In 2014 the United States Air Force, for example, had two thousand fighter jets, whereas at the end of the Cold War it owned 4155. The specialist bomber force has also fallen by more than 50 per cent. The Ukraine crisis may once more have awakened interest in Nato plans for reinforcing vulnerable members to the east, but it arrived at a time when draw-downs to US combat forces had just removed the last American tanks from Europe. Two small brigade combat teams (one in Germany, the other in Italy, totalling thirty thousand troops with their enabling and HQ units) are all that now remains of a US Army force in Europe that twenty-five years ago numbered 210,000 and could field five thousand tanks.

So while the public perception remains that the US

is the last military superpower, when members of Congress and others called in the summer of 2014 for Poland and the Baltic republics to be reinforced with troops it prompted the question, which ones, exactly? A few hundred paratroopers were sent from the US to exercise in Poland, and any larger move to help a threatened European country would likely involve the airborne divisions that now form America's contingency force for the entire globe.

When one looks at the cumulative effect of all this trimming, particularly on the European countries that are much further down the road with it, it can be stark, even comical. General Sir Richard Shirreff, who, until the summer of 2014, was the senior non-American officer in Nato, puts it with brutal frankness: 'European countries have effectively disarmed themselves.' General Shirreff says there is no country in the alliance that could now assemble an armoured division (more than fifteen thousand troops and two hundred-plus tanks) for action in Europe in less than six to twelve months. To my surprise, he does not even think the US would be capable of doing it any faster.

In terms of the number of people it has in the forces, the UK now ranks thirty-first in the world. For the Royal Air Force, a mission by six bombers (as flown by Tornados from RAF Marham in Norfolk to Libya in 2011) is about the limit of its long-range strike capability. For the 'Submarine Service', having two hunter-killer submarines at sea – to cover the entire globe – is now normal, and it could easily fall to a single boat in a few years' time as older *Trafalgar*-class vessels are retired.

With smaller European countries, the token nature of their deployable armed forces is even more obvious. Keeping several F-16 fighters in Kandahar to support the alliance in Afghanistan was pretty much the entire Belgian air force's mission, and four Leopard tanks that of the Danish 'armoured corps'. When one of those Leopards was damaged by an IED in Helmand Province, the Danish tank contingent suffered a prolonged 25 per cent reduction in capability.

Going back to British power at the time of that Spithead Naval Review, the Royal Navy has fallen from third in the world in 1977 to a position somewhat further down the league table. Entire capabilities, many of which would be most useful to the defence of the British Isles, have been lost. There were nineteen diesel-electric submarines back then; there are none now. The maritime patrol air force, then made up of Nimrods, has been scrapped. Reshaping the UK armed forces for 'power projection' – or, to put it crudely, for the Bush/Blair wars – during the late 1990s has left them singularly ill-equipped to protect their own homeland now that the British public has apparently decided that it wants no more of this type of expeditionary warfare.

As for the frigate and destroyer force, that basic yardstick of naval capability, the fleet of nineteen now run by the UK puts it behind China, France, India, Japan, and South Korea, and only just ahead of Germany and Italy. These were all nations whose naval power was eclipsed by that of the Royal Navy in 1977. Many may feel entirely unconcerned by the change. The contempt for Britain's post-imperial delusions runs deep in the commentariat. If cutting the navy down to size is a good way of signalling that Britain is a different country, why not?

Delighting, though, in the decline of a once-proud,

world-beating organisation ignores both history and geography. If the UK, as the world's sixth-largest economy, is heavily dependent on sea trade, should it not be protected? This is the first generation in centuries to step back from a commitment to sea power, a period of history that spans times when the nation was in imminent danger of invasion as well as those when Albion seemed impregnable, times when Britain stood alone and others when it had strong alliances. Yet through all those changing times, it maintained a powerful navy.

The idea that it is safe to step back from this commitment rests on all kinds of assumptions: the protective power of the United States; the technological superiority of the West; and the absence of direct threats to the security of the British Isles. Yet global politics, tilted by economic crisis, radicalisation and the growth of new powers, is shifting very fast. And in this sense, the picture presented above of Britain's declining defence capability, or even more specifically of the Royal Navy and its surface fleet, are simply examples of a much larger phenomenon concerning 'the West', which for the sake of argument I will use here simply as an alternative for Nato and its members.

That fleet which I craned my neck to watch from a crowded ferry back in 1977 no longer exists. So far, so obvious. But the strategic assumptions that led politicians to send *Leander*-class frigates or the *Oberon*-class submarines to the scrapyard are now unsafe. And among these beliefs, one of the least safe is the idea that the West can keep an unassailable military edge for the foreseeable future.

2

Force Multipliers

In the manufacturers' videos for modern weapons, the term 'force multiplier' is often used to explain why buying fewer, vastly more expensive models is a good idea. It could be a ship like the Aegis cruiser, which can track hundreds of incoming missiles simultaneously, or a helicopter that can engage a dozen enemy tanks from behind a ridge. But the logic that the shrinkage of Western defences can be offset by the introduction of ever more advanced weapons is flawed. In fact, the intimate relationship between the arms makers and bureaucracies like the Pentagon may be accelerating rather than mitigating the decline of Western forces relative to their potential adversaries. There is also evidence that many countries outside the Nato bloc have found ways to procure more effective weaponry.

The history of the F-22 Raptor, an American air-superiority fighter jet, shows well what's going wrong. Originally intended to replace 650 aircraft, the production line was shut down after only 182 (or 196, including prototypes) had been made. Raptor is a 'fifth generation' fighter that combines stealth capability with agility and capable sensors. But it is also fifth generation in the sense of its makers and US Air Force users having had successive learning experiences in how to get a major project commissioned and keep it from the budgetary knife. Among other black arts, this involves over-promising on performance and spreading the work across as many legislators' districts as possible – in this case in forty-six states.

There can be little doubt that the F-22 has been colossally expensive. There are many different ways of measuring a fighter's cost, starting with the basic airframe (bereft even of engines) and ending with the entire through-life cost including maintenance, upgrades and training infrastructure. By median estimates, the USAF's F-22s have cost $377 million *each*, but the through-life cost estimates take that to over $670 million per plane. By the time the plug was finally pulled on the project, some members of Congress who were trying to keep it going were doing so in the face of public pleas by the Secretary of Defense to kill it.

In one sense, the F-22 represents the technological supremacy of the United States, for there can be little doubt that it is a very advanced aircraft, deployed many years ahead of what any adversary could have achieved. But the plane also shows how even a defence budget the size of America's can be sucked dry producing small numbers of fragile platforms of dubious value in combat.

As to whether the Raptor really is a world-beating aircraft, that can be argued endlessly by its partisans and detractors. But it is hard to escape the conclusion that, however good an individual F-22 might be on a given day (when it's working), the project as a whole represents a significant loss of capability for the US Air Force. Why?

The first and most obvious point is that replacing dozens of fighter squadrons with just seven of the F-22s reduces the US Air Force's ability to patrol airspace. It doesn't matter if a new jet is super-agile or can engage the enemy at twice the range (debatable in this case anyway), if it costs so much that you can only have a handful of squadrons, net capability is reduced. If, for example, America held back some squadrons for home defence, it is unlikely that it could deploy more than a few dozen Raptors in any confrontation with China, with its hundreds of fighter jets. In such a battle, as one 2008 Rand Corporation simulation showed, even if an F-22 force hit every target it engaged, it would run out of air-to-air missiles, leaving the skies to the Chinese fighters.

It gets worse. The F-22, in order to retain its stealth capabilities, carries fewer air-to-air missiles than the planes it replaced. The maintenance of its stealth performance requires a complex regime that reduces further the number of aircraft available for combat and means that it may never meet the type of through-life improvement in performance and reliability that previous generations of military aircraft (such as the Royal Air Force Typhoon, for example) have shown.

A 2014 report by the US General Accounting Office showed that a ten-year effort to improve the Raptor's 'availability rate' (i.e., the number that are fully combat-capable at any time) had failed, and that it still hovered at around 60 per cent rather than the desired 70 per cent. Older types of aircraft, such as the F-16 or F/A-18, regularly achieve 70 or 80 per cent availability rate.

So really, the whole colossal F-22 investment buys around a hundred fully functional jets on any given day. Far from 'force multiplication', the Pentagon approach sees force division, even if an individual Raptor may be a more formidable piece of technology than the six F-15s it replaced or any MiG or Sukhoi it might fly against.

The acquisition costs have been so high and the numbers of stealth aircraft bought so low that the remaining inventory of US Air Force types has become very old. In 2014 the average age of the US fighter force (and the F-22 is part of that calculation) is twenty-four years, and of bombers thirty-eight years. Much of the fleet has long since exceeded its design life. Many F-15C fighters, for example, have been reported to have flown around ten thousand hours, three times what they were designed and built to do. With low ordering rates for their super-expensive replacements, and the near-obsolescence of much of the American fighter force, numbers could decline dramatically – by hundreds – in the next ten years.

As for the fleet available for long-range strikes against countries with sophisticated air defences: it is tiny. At the time of writing, the US has a force of 158 bombers, including ancient B-52s, B-1s and stealth B-2s. With the retirement of the B-52, this force is expected to fall below one hundred over the coming decade. Of these, there are just nineteen B-2s, the plane still believed capable of penetrating advanced defences such as those of Russia and China. Yet the B-2, so colossally expensive to procure that at the time it was calculated that an aircraft of the same weight made of solid gold would have been cheaper, has also suffered from many maintenance and avail-ability issues. Experts reckon that the advanced US bomber force (i.e., B-2s) available for operations on any given day is around six aircraft. This is the type of cold fact that needs to be considered very carefully by anyone who assumes that US military dominance is here to stay. And if, in the opening phase of a conflict against a nation with substantial air defences such as North Korea, the USAF was to lose some B-2s, imagine the consequences for the Pentagon's ability to keep fighting. Planes like the B-2 or F-22 are no longer in production, so replacements could take many years to make.

Acquisitions like the B-2 or F-22 go at least some of the way to explaining why America's defence capabilities are in decline despite the fact that the Pentagon spends, in dollar terms, substantially more than it did at the end of the Cold War. The US, like many European countries, gets terrible value for money in this area, and that is due in part to 'defence inflation', the rate at which weapons purchases increase in cost being far greater than price rises in the wider economy. So even though the Obama administration has, in response to criticism, revisited some of its cuts early in 2015, the sums involved are not big enough to change the underlying trend. A new plan to keep the USA's nuclear-weapon stockpile effective and safe, for example, would consume three-quarters of the $48 billion annual uplift being offered by the White House – and that's before the cost of replacing hugely expensive systems like strategic bombers or fighter jets has even been considered.

The ownership costs of stealth jets notwithstanding, many of America's allies have now bought into another fifth-generation fighter, the F-35 or Lightning II. Here too work-share has been spread across many congressional districts and friendly countries in order to underscore its economic benefits. And in some ways the F-35 represents an even clearer example of defence procurement black arts than the F-22. It is a multi-role aircraft that replaces several types: standard play for the weapons salesman particularly when pitching to smaller countries. The F-35 was also brought into service before its development was finished, a tactic called 'concurrency' in the Pentagon, which has had the effect of meaning that every improvement made to the aircraft requires the recall and retrofitting of all the jets already with squadrons. At time of writing, none of the dozens of planes that have been delivered to squadrons is yet fit for operational service.

Along with the different roles (the F-35B variant's ability to land vertically, for instance) comes engineering compromise, so much so that many experts believe the F-35 is far less agile in air-to-air combat than the F-16s it will replace in many countries, or indeed the F-22. One Australian politician, reviewing computer-simulated dogfights with Chinese Sukhois, remarked sourly that the F-35s had been 'clubbed like baby seals'.

Reducing the number of aircraft types can save a great deal of money in support costs, but it also increases certain risks. Britain, for example, retired the Harrier as part of its 2010 Strategic Defence and Security Review. Both it and the Tornado are to be replaced by F-35s. But what happens if the delays to the F-35, which are already running into years, extend further, to when the Tornados have passed their service life? And how capable will the new jet be at launching the advanced ground attack weapons used by the existing planes?

Although the answers to these questions are debated by the Ministry of Defence and its critics, there seems to be little doubt that for quite some time (roughly from 2015 to 2020) there will be significant 'capability gaps' for the UK, ranging from the ability to operate fast jets from its new aircraft carriers to not being able to launch some of its more advanced weapons. Barring the cancellation of the F-35, these gaps will eventually be closed in years to come, but the range of air missions that the UK can perform in the meantime will be limited.

The responsibility for this type of procurement rests not just with industry but with senior officers, many of whom have come to regard the replacement of 'platforms' – the high-priced prestige weapons such as fighters or warships – as vital to the future of their branch of the forces. It has long been the case that these spending pledges have been pursued at the expense of almost all other aspects of producing war-winning armed forces, from training the operators to buying sufficient advanced weapons to be used from them. More than twenty years ago, during a briefing on the RAF's new Typhoon fighter, I was told that buying a respectable stock of missiles and other weapons could cost three and a half times as much as the aircraft itself. Since the number of squadrons in an air force or ships in a fleet is easily measurable, but the quantity of missiles or smart bombs in its storage bunkers far less visible, this has frequently been an area of economies.

During the 2011 operation in Libya, British short-comings showed themselves in several ways. HMS *Westminster*, a frigate sent to operate close to the North African coast, reportedly carried just four missiles for its Sea Wolf missile system. As this would have been its prime self-defence weapon if attacked by Libyan air-craft or missiles, the risks of entering combat should have been obvious. The RAF also found the campaign taxing, as its stocks of two advanced weapons, the Brimstone missile and Paveway IV bomb, came close to running out. The number of these weapons used during the campaign (230 and nine hundred respec-tively) shows how small the inventories must have been in the first place for the air strikes on Colonel Gaddafi's forces to produce this problem. The Royal Navy's stock of Tomahawk cruise missiles was revealed at the time as just sixty-four, twelve of which were fired at Libyan targets.

To give some sense of how small these stocks of precision weapons are, the entire UK inventory of Brimstone and Paveway IV would have been sufficient to destroy the equipment of just one of the dozens of Saddam Hussein's armoured brigades fielded during the 1991 Gulf War, or the entire stock of Tomahawks to neutralise one of his larger airfields. And as the Ministry of Defence saw during the 2011 Libyan operation, a re-order for advanced weapons like Brimstone can take many months, if not years, to deliver, meaning there is no choice but to switch weapons or give up in the meantime.

The strategic advantages that might accrue from the possession of advanced weapons have been further undermined by the effects of years of spending cuts on the servicing of equipment and training of crews. Like the issues with precision weapons described above, cutbacks in maintenance or training are not easily visible and the culture of official secrecy has helped to disguise just how deeply these economies have harmed defence capabilities. Until the F-35 enters service, the

Typhoon fighter remains the most advanced jet in the inventory of the partners that built it (the UK, Germany, Italy and Spain).

In the autumn of 2014, Jane's reported that of Germany's 109 Typhoons, only forty-two were considered combat-ready. Some thirty-five jets were in long-term maintenance, or 'hangar queens' in air force parlance, with a further thirty-two requiring work to get them fully functional. Spain's readiness was believed to be even worse. Of thirty-nine Typhoons, only six were reported to be fully functional in late 2014. These few jets, based at two airfields, have become Spain's last remaining protection against a variety of threats ranging from hostile-state air incursions to a 9/11-style attack by hijackers. It is easy to see that with a country the size of Spain effectively putting its trust in a handful of planes and pilots, any mishap in terms of maintenance, pilot availability or the delayed identification of an airborne threat would leave the country's cities quite defenceless. The RAF, in comparison, has around twenty-five of its one hundred Typhoons in long-term servicing, and can muster a few dozen fully serviceable aircraft across the four squadrons equipped with them.

While the British story in terms of advanced jet readiness may be better than that of many other countries, the army's tank force has been damaged by underinvestment and the long Helmand campaign. It has emerged that only around thirty-six of two hundred Challenger tanks were fully operational in the summer of 2014. When Britain chose to send a single armoured battle group (around one thousand men, forty-five Warrior infantry combat vehicles and a couple of dozen Challenger tanks) to Poland that autumn, it had considerable difficulty assembling the vehicles to do so. Senior army officers have told me that the vehicles were badly mothballed during the Afghan campaign and required far more work to get them operational than anyone had imagined.

Indications of a different kind of vulnerability emerged in the Royal Navy at the same time. It became public that the service's engineering branch was so depleted by resignations and staff cuts that some ships could not put to sea. A deal was done with the US Coast Guard for the loan of thirty-six engineers to address the problem. Since such specialists cannot be trained quickly, the shortage of critical skills can pose a long-term problem for Western armed forces.

As with new fighter jets, the lesson with guided missiles, equipment maintenance and skills shortages is that while Nato countries can undoubtedly produce the world's most advanced weapons, they generally can afford so few, and have such difficulty keeping them battle-ready, that any sustained combat could prove problematic. During the long deployments in Iraq and Afghanistan, the US and other Nato members used 'smart weapons' at a slow and predictable rate, re-ordering from manufacturers as circumstances dictated. But in a conflict between states, they could find themselves seriously embarrassed. Since the mid-1990s, the assumption in many Nato defence ministries has been that this was an acceptable risk, given the collapse of the Soviet Union and the belief that the re-emergence of any significant threat to the alliance's members would take some time, perhaps a decade or more, which would allow for rearmament in the meantime.

Even so, there are other respects in which the

Western technological edge may be misunderstood or overestimated. One such area is the increasing adoption of Unmanned Aerial Vehicles (UAVs), or drones. The idea that the drone is a particularly advanced or indeed immoral weapon rests on the popular misconception that it can seek out and kill targets without having humans in the loop; that it is a true robot.

In reality, the growing use of UAVs during the US-led 'War on Terror' campaigns stemmed largely from their cheapness. The economies are not just the result of lower acquisition costs, since the combat drone has its origin in the radio-controlled model aeroplanes adapted by the Israelis in the 1980s, but also in making 'long-linger surveillance' far less expensive. A UAV, armed or not, can circle its target for many hours, consuming far less fuel than its manned equivalent, doing so less obtrusively and requiring 'pilots' who cost a fraction of the price to train and can change shifts at the desk from which they control the plane while it is aloft. In some ways a UAV is the exact opposite of a procurement like the F-35: it was bought quickly and very cheaply to do a defined job in a benign environment.

Drones are very low-tech. They are so easy to build that many emerging military powers (including Iran, for example) have done so, and even insurgent movements such as Hamas and ISIS have demonstrated a basic UAV capability. These platforms have distinct limitations, though. While they can orbit above the range of small arms used by insurgents, they can easily be shot down by anti-aircraft weapons. The data links used to control the aircraft and transmit its images can also be hacked or jammed, or simply lost if the aircraft executes too violent a manoeuvre.

In trying to prepare a future generation of drones for more demanding roles, designers are giving them stealth capabilities, greater autonomy and higher weapon payloads. The British Taranis is one such plane, and the US Navy has been conducting trials flying its N-UCAS prototype from aircraft carriers. Part of the logic advanced for the latter is that it should have a far longer range than F/A-18 jets, making it able to hit targets such as shore-based cruise missile launchers (of the type extensively fielded by China) that might endanger the carrier.

Whether the growing number of UAVs in Nato

service demonstrates that these countries have the edge, or simply that they prefer cheap systems that do not risk the lives of pilots, is open to debate. The capture of a CIA RQ-170 Sentinel by Iran late in 2011, however, should give pause for thought to anyone who thinks such aircraft could give Western forces the advantage in any inter-state conflict. Iran claimed to have overridden the American drone's control system so that it could be landed intact. Whether or not Iran actually achieved this feat, there is evidence both that the Sentinel's stealth design did not protect it from detection and that the Iranians may have caused its crash landing by jamming its control signals rather than actually hacking them.

There is one last trend to note in defence technology in Nato countries since the end of the Cold War. As budgets have declined and the tendency to label other countries as adversaries has faded, the export of previously sensitive technologies has been permitted in an attempt to keep defence industries from entering a catastrophic decline.

Just as the super-rich of the world's emerging economic powers have gone shopping for high-end property in Mayfair, Neuilly or Verbier, so their governments have embarked on major spending sprees on weaponry. In some countries, such as India and Russia, a big emphasis has been placed on developing home-grown manufacturing and technologies. Others, such as Saudi Arabia or the United Arab Emirates, have signed huge contracts with Western defence firms.

Even those with big arms production plants of their own have gone to the West when high-end technology or techniques have been needed. India ordered a dozen of the advanced C-17 transport planes (more of this type than the RAF operates) from the United States, and Russia commissioned two *Mistral*-class landing ships from France.

In some places, Western countries have assisted emerging military powers in acquiring technologies that were previously closely guarded. So there are now many owners of spy satellites (Israel, Japan, and India, for example), drones, advanced guided missiles, and even in certain cases nuclear technology (India and Israel), who have benefited from the transfer of sensitive know-how.

Countries like Saudi Arabia and the UAE have come to rival Western armed forces in the scale of their orders from Western firms and complexity of the technology involved. Saudi Arabia has taken delivery of eighty-four F-15E Strike Eagle aircraft from the US and recently announced the intention to spend €12 billion with Germany acquiring a submarine fleet. The Emirates, meanwhile, are acquiring spy satellites from France, Patriot air-defence missiles from the US and a wide range of other sophisticated armaments.

The ability to mount networked warfare – in which sensors pass a real-time picture of the enemy to advanced combat aircraft equipped with precision weapons – is increasingly shared by non-Western countries. Israel has had its own satellites, drones and smart weaponry for years. Now countries from the UAE to India, China and Russia are deploying the same capabilities. And whereas the US could once threaten to deny access to the global-positioning satellites used by ships and planes, or the weapons they have launched, to fix their exact position (and hence improve accuracy dramatically), Russia and China have each deployed their own satellite positioning systems – GLONASS and BeiDou respectively. As for the original American GPS, civilian spin-offs such as satnav systems are now so widely available that non-state groups such as Hamas or the Iranian-backed militias in Iraq used them to improve the accuracy of their attacks.

What all of these trends amount to is a qualitative as well as a quantitative erosion of Western superiority. This is relevant less to the conflicts of the past decade – against insurgents in Iraq and Afghanistan, for example – than it could be to those of the next ten or twenty years. It is not just a matter of confrontation with one of the world's big emerging powers – Russia, China or India. It could also be a game-changer if militant forces gained control of one of the countries that have recently invested so heavily in military hardware. Some modern US-supplied weapons were seized by ISIS in taking over northern Iraq. But their haul is trivial compared with what might happen if the government of Saudi Arabia or Egypt were to succumb to a similar type of enemy.

3

Kneel or Starve

A couple of years into the Syrian civil war, reports emerged that the regime of President Bashar al-Assad had presented residents in a war-torn suburb of Damascus with a simple choice: submit or die. It cropped up in various reporters' accounts, though the wording was sometimes different: 'kneel or die' and 'submit or starve' were among them. I wondered whether regime troops had really painted signs with such slogans, or indeed, more importantly, whether a government was genuinely prepared to tell its people it would rather see them starve to death than persist in their rebellion.

In June 2014 the Vice News website provided some substance to the reports. It told the story of Moadamiya, south-west of Damascus, where hundreds had died in the various attempts by the Assad forces to regain control. Accompanying the article was a photo showing a slogan painted on a wall close to the neighbourhood, saying 'Kneel or Starve'. A regime soldier is walking by, and the official Syrian government flag hangs beside the slogan.

Moadamiya had been the target of one of the Sarin chemical-weapons attacks in August 2013. It had also been the scene of countless air strikes, artillery bombardments and attempts by government infantry to drive out the rebels. By the time of writing, despite the determination to capture the place, none of these efforts had succeeded. But then in the summer of 2014, details emerged of the desperate situation in Yarmouk, a huge Palestinian refugee camp near the Syrian capital that had been under siege by the president's forces since late 2012. When UN humanitarian workers were briefly allowed in they saw scenes of utter destruction and of heart-breaking desperation among those who remained there. For of a pre-war population of half a million, only around thirty thousand were left. Resistance had largely collapsed. Here, too, were signs saying 'Kneel or Starve'.

The Assad government had adopted a policy of starvation, blockading these neighbourhoods of food, and, in places, it seems to have worked for them. These tactics were just part of a war of hideous brutality that has driven an estimated nine million people from their homes, with three million becoming refugees outside Syria's borders. By the late summer of 2014 the death toll had topped two hundred thousand. Nothing is off limits, apparently, from dousing people with nerve agents to starvation, barrel bombs (home-made kegs of explosive dropped, unguided, onto rebel-held neighbourhoods), the wiping out of entire families, and – a particular favourite among the jihadist rebels – beheadings by the hundred.

The appetite for war, and indeed the ability to endure suffering, varies dramatically in different countries and cultures around the world. Many in Europe could barely understand the British desire to join the US-led campaigns in Iraq and Afghanistan, putting it down to Anglo-Saxon solidarity or post-imperial hubris. The experience of those difficult campaigns, and the loss of more than six hundred soldiers in them, was enough to convince most Britons that they should steer clear of foreign crises.

Government ministers blamed the loss of the 2013 parliamentary vote about intervention in Syria on an 'Iraq effect'. And General Sir Nick Houghton, Chief of the Defence Staff, highlighted 'a creeping aversion to risk in the employment of our armed forces' as, potentially, 'the most damaging of all' challenges facing them.

Even the US, tallying up the colossal cost of its interventions in Iraq and Afghanistan while dealing with economic crisis at home, appears markedly less ready to employ military force. This has led to repeated attacks from the Republican right on President Barack Obama that he has abrogated American leadership and given a green light to dictators, terrorists and adventurers around the world.

'War weariness or maybe better termed "war wariness" is a significant factor in America,' according to General Stan McChrystal, who commanded US special mission forces in Iraq and the overall Nato effort in Afghanistan. The challenge to America resulting from these missions, he told me, 'is a rejection of perceived failure or long-term frustration. Colonial powers were often willing to fight extended wars to maintain possessions, [but] it is harder to maintain American focus and commitment when either our partners appear uncommitted or unreliable or if success is unlikely or very far off.' All of this produced a desire to walk away – from Iraq in particular – so strong that it was hardly in the US interest. In the summer of 2014, after Islamist militants took over much of the country, forcing President Obama to engage 'Reverse', sending troops back to Iraq. Even so, the new effort to help Iraq's government and strike against the self-proclaimed Islamic State has come with emphatic attempts to guarantee that ground forces will not be used, and distinct limits on the air and other forces committed.

In some respects Obama's policy has resembled that of Bill Clinton's presidency. Both Democrats were prepared to use military force but tried to confine it to air power, with specific promises at the outset of military action (Clinton on Kosovo, Obama on Libya and the

2014 Iraq intervention) not to put US boots on the ground. But to characterise Barack Obama as a wimp ignores his willingness, to put it crudely, to kill people – with drones, manned air strikes and special operations forces. He's done it in Pakistan, Somalia, Yemen, Libya and Iraq.

What Obama has been reluctant to do, in marked contrast to Clinton, is take on other states. The earlier president used thousands of air strikes against Slobodan Milošević's Yugoslavia and even more bombs were dropped on Saddam's Iraq, where for several years substantial US air forces policed no-fly zones. President Obama was most reluctant to attack Syria, which, with its substantial air defences, would have required a commitment similar in size to that of the Yugoslav campaign. When striking Libya in 2011, a far weaker adversary than Syria, Mr Obama made sure that after initial strikes most of the burden of killing Gaddafi's forces was left to other Nato allies. The Obama policy, and it has largely been in tune with US public opinion, has been to avoid protracted action, avoid state opponents wherever possible and to conduct strikes against the type of irregular or terrorist groups that might attack Americans. Even those actions that have been launched have risked few American lives (or none at all in the case of drone strikes), and required only a small part of the war machine at his disposal.

The 9/11 attacks produced an aberrant moment in America's declining willingness to intervene militarily abroad. It was a significant blip in that downward trend which, although it did not resemble wars like Vietnam or Korea in its scale or costs, did require considerable sacrifice. More than 6700 people were lost in the 'War on Terror' – after years in which the US had been characterised by many as increasingly 'casualty averse' – and the bill could easily reach $2 trillion. The reality of trying to nation-build or buy a security 'breathing space' for the US-installed governments in Baghdad and Kabul was so ugly, as well as frustratingly difficult, that it has left many Americans yearning for casualty-free 'solutions' like those advocated by Mr Obama's Democratic predecessor. The Clinton White House was deemed to be so reluctant to hazard American ground troops following the loss of forty-three in Somalia (1992–3) that it stood by and did nothing to stop the genocide in Rwanda.

In 1995, soon after that African tragedy, strategist Edward N. Luttwak wrote of 'post-heroic warfare', a new state of affairs in which the ability to use force for grand state objectives at the cost of huge casualties had disappeared in Western nations, among other reasons because developed societies spawned smaller families. 'The loss of a youngster in combat, however tragic,' Luttwak wrote of earlier centuries, was 'fundamentally less unacceptable than for today's families, with their one, two, or at most three children.'

The other great societal change that has overcome Western countries since 1945 is that they have forgotten what it is like to feel under existential threat. During the Cold War, a German politician thinking back to a childhood memory of a flattened Hamburg or Dresden, or a British one who considered the Blitz and the importance of the Battle of Britain in the national psyche, could readily project what a cataclysm the failure of nuclear deterrence might produce. This made it vital to avoid war at almost any price. Although many proxy conflicts, such as Vietnam or Afghanistan, were conducted during the Cold War, the need to avoid any face-to-face confrontation with the Soviet Union or China made Western politicians extremely reluctant to use their forces in many situations.

One excellent example of this mentality occurred some years after the fall of the Berlin Wall, when Nato forces were racing towards Pristina airport in Kosovo. When it was discovered that a column of Russian troops were trying to beat them to it, the US Supreme Allied Commander, General Wesley Clark, contacted the Nato corps commander, the British General Sir Mike Jackson (both of them soldiers defined by the Cold War), telling him to stop the Russians and implying that force might be necessary. Jackson refused, telling Clark, 'I'm not going to start the Third World War.'

For the public more widely, the end of the Cold War marked an opportunity to escape the idea of Mutually Assured Destruction, and as the Second World War generation started to pass, memories of smashed European cities began to fade. This has produced a paradox, a situation in which most of the European public has been conditioned by education and popular culture to be repulsed by war, yet has little experience of it. That lack of direct understanding leads them to embark on limited military expeditions, such as Nato's campaign in Afghanistan, both with unrealistic ideas about what might be achieved and, for many people, without considering the consequences of what conflict on a larger scale, if it were to return to Europe, might mean to their personal security. And when people do consider the possible blowback, for example in terms of terrorist acts on the streets of their city, they often expect their governments to be able to provide complete security.

History has given Americans quite different sensibilities. In the first place, they have no folk memory of being bombed, as the Germans or British do, or indeed occupied like the French or Poles. So when the 9/11 attacks happened, the historical comparison that many reached for was Pearl Harbor, since it was the only vaguely similar attack on US territory in living memory. But the eastern seaboard has never been attacked in the same way, unless you include Britain's burning down of the White House during the War of 1812, and so the reaction to this evidence of their own vulnerability was even more extreme than anything that happened in Europe, say, after the al-Qaeda-inspired attacks in Madrid and London. The American response to this trauma was violent, but it was also successful in the sense of preventing, to date, the launch of any similar assault from overseas on American soil.

The 'War on Terror', a moment of rage and revenge, passed and now it is safe to assume that, absent another disaster on the scale of 9/11, many Americans would prefer to step back from the role of global policeman in general, and particularly from anything that involves a long-term commitment to 'stability operations' or nation-building. Some of the senior American military leaders I consulted argue that the American public still supports the idea of being global top dog in terms of hard power, but polls and other research suggest the public is very reluctant to see ground troops or large-scale interventions right now. These attitudes are felt even more deeply by European countries, so much so that some could not even bring themselves to support the US when it was on the warpath after 9/11.

More than a decade after that trauma, Western societies are still struggling to calibrate their reaction to security threats. The willingness to use force against small non-state groups remains quite high – for example in US or UK opinion polls at the time that they started bombing Islamic State militants in Iraq. Yet a widespread belief that such campaigns are 'wars' has led to a profound misreading of what war can mean, in terms of its cost to a society. Losses in Baghdad or Helmand, however shocking, remain trivial compared with those of previous conflicts, and similarly, the killing by terrorists of dozens of people – such as in London in July 2005 – may be a tragedy, but it's no Blitz.

'I'm sceptical of the war-weariness theory because the British people have not been at war,' says General Sir Richard Shirreff, Nato's second most senior officer until 2014. 'Yes, the impact of pictures of flag-covered coffins being driven through Wootton Bassett has been powerful, but in all other respects there has been no impact on most people's lives at all.' The political realities of the moment, he argues, have led Western leaders to adopt the emotional rhetoric of remembrance or solidarity with the armed forces while continuing to cut them: 'While we see leaders like Cameron wrapping themselves in a flag of sentimentality about the armed forces, and uttering trite clichés about our brave boys and girls, he will readily apply cuts to capability with a cynical disregard to the consequences for defence.'

Similar views pervade the armed forces leadership across the Atlantic. Admiral Bill Fallon, who commanded US forces in the Pacific and then the Middle East, notes that it became a familiar formulation in the Pentagon that 1 per cent of the US economy paid for the long post-9/11 campaigns, and 1 per cent of the population fought them. 'As a percentage of people, the number involved in this is minimal,' he told me, 'and they are getting minimal support here, they are getting lip service, and that really bothers me.'

However, in prosecuting these 'expeditionary' conflicts many senior officers, as they have tried to stave off spending cuts, have not themselves been immune to the manipulation of strategic threats for their own bureaucratic interest. The decision to commit the British Army to Helmand Province in 2006 is now widely perceived to have been a strategic error, yet at the time the decisions were taken senior officers justified them to me both in terms of preventing Tony

Blair from sending more troops to Iraq, which they already regarded as a lost cause, and of justifying the future strength of the British Army. In truth, strategic elites throughout the Western world came to regard 'war' – in the sense of a contest between entire societies, using all the means at their disposal – as a thing of the past after the Cold War, and to give credence to the idea that 'contingency' or 'stability' operations were actually what twenty-first-century 'war' looked like. Developments in Russia and China are now forcing military leaders to think in much more traditional terms about what a full-scale conflict might involve.

Despite recent events in Ukraine and the Middle East, many senior military people worry that Western societies have not registered the scale of the changed environment, in part because their politicians are not ready to make the case for ground interventions or higher defence spending. 'There is a prejudice against decisive military engagement in the wake of the Iraq and Afghan conflicts, exacerbated by a sense of moral disarmament across Europe driven by weak political leadership,' General Sir Peter Wall, UK Chief of the General Staff until 2014, told me. Both the Ukraine crisis and that triggered by the Islamic State's conquest of northern Iraq in June 2014 required a US lead. As for future challenges, the general believes, 'The longer we wait the more significant the problems are likely to be.'

When it comes to the US, the memory of the al-Qaeda attacks on New York and Washington means that the Obama White House is still willing to take the life of terrorists. But the understanding of the huge price to be paid in occupying entire countries means a return to 1990s 'post-heroic' principles and an even greater aversion to tackling state enemies than was exhibited by the Clinton administration.

Where the 'post-heroic' idea falls down is in the notion that economic development, raised living standards and smaller families lead to an abhorrence of war in every society. In fact, the results seem to depend to a great degree on recent history and how it informs a sense of national vulnerability. In one specific case, Israel, it can be argued that even 'Western' societies do not all share the same reluctance to use force on a grand scale and risk significant losses. A poll late on during Israel's 2014 Gaza offensive (which cost around two thousand Palestinian and sixty-seven Israeli lives) showed 87 per cent support for continued military action, and that only 4 per cent believed excessive force had been used. Israel is a singular case, though, and perhaps its willingness to take life is indeed one of the main reasons that it seems increasingly out of kilter with European or even US public opinion.

The more interesting examples are Russia and China. People in both societies have moved away from large families and seen major improvements in their standards of living. In that sense, they have become more like the West. But President Vladimir Putin has found that using the armed forces makes him very popular. The brief 2008 war against Georgia and the 2014 seizure of Crimea boosted his poll ratings considerably. His popularity even survived (at time of writing at least) the bloodier intervention in eastern Ukraine and consequent imposition of Western sanctions. In China, there is a groundswell of popular, nationalistic support for 'giving Japan a lesson' over the islands disputed between the two countries.

In countries like Libya, Iraq or Syria, of course, there is widespread support within particular communities for the use of extreme violence. It may be argued that in these places all order has broken down and a type of anarchy has ensued, and indeed this provides a vital clue to the differences between the attitudes towards using force in European and in other societies. It is less to do with the level of social development or indeed the odd notion still espoused by some Western liberals that democracies do not start wars. The willingness to use force depends in these cases largely on the perceived threat, the sense that your enemies might easily and randomly murder you in bed or on the way to work.

The word 'perceived' is important. In Russia, toying with potent memories of the Second World War, the Kremlin propagated the idea that Ukraine had been taken over by Nazis and its Russian citizens were in danger, so action was imperative. For China, the manipulation of nationalist sentiment against Japan depends crucially on the memory of its 1930s atrocities. In Israel, the apparent security given by the Iron Dome missile defence system or the barrier closing off the West Bank has only limited effect on the national psyche. The sense of being marooned in a sea of homicidal hostility is so deeply ingrained that any hint that these defences are about to be breached – by rockets getting through to Tel Aviv, or people tunnelling under the Gaza fences – can arouse extreme violence.

If the willingness to use force depends crucially on a sense of fear or vulnerability, this also explains the differences between transatlantic Western allies after 9/11. For Americans, the attacks on the World Trade Center and Pentagon were a singular historic event. When talking to British officers in Iraq and Afghanistan about the differences between the UK and US attitudes to risk, casualties, or indeed killing, I was told more than once, 'The difference is that the Americans believe they are at war and we do not.' And as for Britain, it is hard to escape the impression that it was because Tony Blair and his spin doctors saw the need to convince people in the run-up to the Iraq War that Saddam Hussein somehow constituted an immediate and real threat to the country – so that the British public experienced a sense of insecurity similar to that felt by many Americans – that they disastrously overplayed their hand.

America's sense of vulnerability has not entirely vanished since its withdrawal from Iraq and disengagement in Afghanistan. It still feels it could be targeted by terrorist groups, which is why certain types of counter-terrorist spending have defied the general cuts to defence in the federal budget. A similar but smaller-scale phenomenon is present in the UK and several other European countries. The US Air Force may have slashed the number of fighter squadrons it operates, but America has built enormous storage centres for the National Security Agency's trawls of global metadata. Britain has half the number of frigates that it did twenty years ago, but MI5 has doubled in size over just about the same period.

These measures, though, have more in common with international law enforcement than fighting wars. Indeed, in its attempts to effect outcomes in ungoverned space (places like Yemen, Somalia, northern Syria or the tribal areas of Pakistan) through drone strikes or special operations, the US has used small numbers of people and suffered few casualties. President George W. Bush's invocation of the old poster 'Wanted Dead or Alive' in the hunt for Osama bin Laden suggested a Wild-West analogy of rough-and-ready solutions for the places beyond the reach of normal laws. It is a campaign conducted by small numbers of volunteers, usually in great secrecy, and therefore little understood by the people at home.

Almost all terrorist events of recent years have also been more comparable to gang crime than war in terms of the damage done to Western societies, with the glaring exception of 9/11 itself. This is likely to change, and it was, among other things, the realisation that groups like al-Qaeda would use weapons of mass destruction if they obtained them that led Bush and Blair to react in such an extreme way. The former top US intelligence analyst Mathew Burrows predicts that 'the next fifteen to twenty years will see a wider spectrum of more accessible instruments of war, especially precision-strike capabilities, cyber instruments, and bioterror weaponry'. The leaking of technology such as GPS or advanced programming and chemistry skills to insurgent or terrorist groups will allow them to do much more damage, he argues.

We are not there yet, and the huge effort made by the US and others to prevent another event on the scale of 9/11 has so far been successful. But the nature of this counter-terrorist campaign may have lulled the public in Western countries into a false sense of security and further distorted their perceptions about what larger-scale collisions between societies might look like. The British papers' description of sending eight RAF Tornado jets to bomb Islamic State militants in the summer of 2014 as 'going to war' gives some idea of how far this distortion has gone. Imagine the shock that would result if those terrorists were able to visit a similar level of force on Britain in response.

There are other models of strife that are also starting to worry Western societies. The Paris terror attacks early in 2015 followed multiple incidents of murder and attempted murder in France by radicalised Islamists. One writer has even characterised what is happening as the 'French Intifada'. Even if that's hype, the possibility of a long-running, low-level anti-terror campaign now seems very real in France. For much of Europe and America, though, there is still a conviction that 'it couldn't happen here', and as long as people feel that sense of security they can avoid all sorts of difficult questions about how far they would go to protect it.

In Syria, of course, there are no such illusions. The tragedy there not only tells us much about the willingness of people who feel under mortal threat to use force in its most extreme forms – including starving to death their former neighbours in the Damascus suburbs. It also shows how the manipulation of fear can create this very situation.

During the early months and years of the Syrian rebellion, regime propaganda constantly tried to rally the loyalty of its citizens by portraying itself as the only alternative to homicidal jihadist fanatics. It played particularly on the fears of minorities such as the Alawites, Christians and Druze that they would be slaughtered by the Sunni majority. In the nightmare that has played out since then, the urbanised Sunnis who had first sided with the regime have largely deserted it. And, across the divide, the sane, moderate-minded Sunnis who opposed the Assad system from the outset have in many places been crushed or murdered by jihadist extremists.

As the country has polarised, and stepped closer to the nightmare conjured up at the outset by the Assad regime, the limits on violence have been removed one by one. Ballistic missiles have been fired at people with small arms. The air force, once held back, had by 2014 been used so frequently that it was often having to augment proper bombs with the home-made 'barrel' variety. Sarin and chlorine have been deployed. Entire cities, such as Aleppo, that were hardly touched in the first year of violence have now been consumed by it.

Could European societies be reduced by strife and fear to this type of medieval violence? The question cannot be answered – at least not in the short term. The bigger issue for the immediate future, just as it has been during the immediate past for the US in Baghdad or Britain in Helmand, is what are Western societies, with their sense of comfortable security, going to do when they encounter people willing to use extreme violence? And, more importantly, what if those belligerent parties are not just small non-state groups, but major powers?

4

The Faltering Giant

Back in 2012, Republican presidential contender Mitt Romney toured the United States with a message that Barack Obama had forfeited American leadership and was taking the country to the dogs. Foreign policy did not form a major plank of the Romney campaign, but he did frequently touch on mounting US debt, unfair competition from countries like China and the sense that America had entered a decline under the Democrats. In a warehouse on the outskirts of Dayton, Ohio the *Newsnight* team filmed one of his hundreds of speeches on the stump.

Romney was no great orator, and his accusations that the president had abandoned America's role in the world hardly brought the house down. But talking to audience members afterwards, it was clear that his remarks about the country counting for less in the world had struck a chord. Indeed, polls during the campaign year showed anything from two-thirds to three-quarters of Americans agreeing to the proposition that the country was less strong than it used to be, or in decline. When Romney was challenged over whom the White House ought to be standing up to, he named Russia, which caused President Obama to ridicule him. But to be fair, Romney was repeating a party line consistently used by John McCain, who ran in 2008, that Vladimir Putin was not to be trusted. Both men consider the Kremlin's subsequent actions in Ukraine to have vindicated their stance.

The issue of decline does not sit easily with American politicians. Republicans insist publicly that the country does not have to slip from its pre-eminent international position, and that strong leadership could reverse the situation. Democrats argue that no failure of direction has occurred, and that Mr Obama's brand of presidency involves interfering less overseas, while avoiding stupid and very costly mistakes such as the invasion of Iraq. Privately, though, neither side seems quite to believe their message; Republicans fret that no amount of assertive leadership could reverse their country's palpable decline, Democrats that the Obama White House has been humiliated by some countries it has reached out to, including Russia.

This underlying sense that it is going downhill has spawned a 'declinist' literature of dozens of books and hundreds of op-ed newspaper articles. It has also stimulated a reaction – from those who dispute the theory, arguing that it is neurotic navel-gazing from a country that is still enormously powerful. In 2012 Robert Kagan wrote persuasively for the *New Republic* on the myth of American decline; so much so that President Obama endorsed it enthusiastically to a group of journalists shortly before his 2012 State of the Union address. Kagan contrasted earlier waves of pessimism with the country's ability to reinvent itself and maintain its global economic position. A 2011 essay by Adam Gopnik in the *New Yorker* deconstructed a batch of recent pessimistic tracts, pointed out that the

'Decline of the West' thesis had been around since Oswald Spengler wrote a book of that title in 1918, and noted that 'the coming catastrophe is always coming, and never quite getting here, so the first job the new declinist book has to do is explain why the previous declinist books were wrong'.

If one were to search for an American Golden Age, many might say it was in the late 1940s or early 1950s. Yet in 1947 Hassan al-Banna, founding ideologue of the Muslim Brotherhood, described the West as 'bankrupt and in decline'. He may, of course, have had the war-shattered societies in Europe uppermost in his mind, but he also regarded the US as morally and spiritually degenerate.

The main arguments of those who doubt the declinist theory of American power are that it still has great military power, as exemplified by its aircraft carrier strike groups and advanced surveillance systems; that its enterprise culture can still produce powerhouses of innovation such as Apple; and that, while enormously indebted, the US is underwritten by China and Gulf states that therefore retain a vested interested in its success.

American primacy cannot be taken for granted in any of these areas. At the heart of this, however, even military leaders recognise the importance of continued economic competitiveness. General Stan McChrystal told me that 'the most fundamental threat to the US comes not from abroad, but from the failure of our education system. Absent the ability to produce skilled workers and an educated electorate, it will be impossible to compete in the world.' For another, Admiral Bill Fallon, the issue of political gridlock in Washington is deeply disturbing. 'Our biggest problem,' he says, 'is really domestic, our seeming inability to clean up our act here at home politically and economically.'

Maybe, given the emotions evoked and the subjectivity of many of the arguments, it is better to stick to the empirical. Of those aspects of life in which the US is still regarded as top dog, innovation and entrepreneurial flair are in the best shape, notwithstanding the widespread concerns about BRICs – the emerging economies of Brazil, Russia, India and China – or the longer-term anxiety spelt out by General McChrystal. However, it is possible to argue that the US economy has only maintained its current position by deficit spending and by pump priming its banking sector through the money-printing process known as quantitative easing.

There can be no dispute that the national debt is enormous and has reached unprecedented levels, though the argument remains active about whether this binds America's rivals to the country's continued success or exposes the country to the possibility of blackmail. At the time of writing, the US national debt has reached nearly $18 trillion, or $18,000 billion. Since the start of the economic crisis six years ago, it has nearly doubled. China holds $1268 billion of the total, and one declinist theory holds that, in the event of an international crisis, China might be able to pressure the US by refusing to buy any more of its government debt. But this idea has drawn sceptical reactions from many, who argue that China bringing down the American economy would be enormously damaging to its own. Another thesis – and more relevant, in my view – is that the pile of federal IOUs has grown so vast that simply servicing the interest on the debt ($415 billion in 2013) will become increasingly problematic. These interest payments, equivalent to two-thirds of the Pentagon's annual bill, have been kept 'manageable' because of historically low interest rates. But if this changes, the competition to sell government paper intensifies and the US has to pay more to borrow, there is a very real possibility of the rising interest burden crushing federal spending across the board.

Quantitative easing, or QE, has also been used in the UK, where by the time of writing it had cost the Bank of England £375 billion, or equivalent to around twelve times the annual defence budget. It's worth making one other point about this huge financial stimulus, and that is that public opinion accepted the colossal but unproductive creation of money to help banks with little dissent, whereas a more orthodox 1930s type of job-creation scheme, either to build more national infrastructure or indeed to reinvest in defence, would have been a political impossibility. Yet while the architects of QE insist it has allowed the US and UK to avoid falling into the deep recession experienced by many Eurozone countries, there is much debate among economists about what the project has in fact achieved. At the same time, QE has added enormously to the liabilities accrued by US and UK central banks.

As for those other yardsticks of superiority, US naval power is unarguably in decline. Whereas 1980s advocates built America's fleet towards 'the six-hundred-ship navy', it was half that size by 2009, and the planners are now assuming a 220 to 240-ship fleet by 2030. The number of aircraft carriers, currently ten, could be expected to fall to seven or eight by that year, which, when factoring in refits and the number of escort vessels available, could leave the US Navy with just four or five deployable globally, which could mean committing more than two or three aircraft carriers to a single specific emergency would become very problematic. So the US Navy is and will remain powerful, but that needs to be measured against the six carrier groups used during the Gulf War in 1991.

The US Navy may remain the world's most powerful fleet, but its reach will be increasingly limited, and stretched across global commitments. Carrier aviation is, however, arguably the most impressive of America's military capabilities and the number of carriers has itself become a totemic estimate of American military superiority in some quarters. But as a currency, the US Navy carrier group has become somewhat debased. During the Cold War, when sailing within striking distance of an enemy coast, these behemoths were often escorted on Nato exercises by six to ten cruisers, destroyers and frigates. It would be hard for America to assemble more than a couple of such groups now.

These days, the US Navy carrier air wings are a little smaller too, at around seventy-five aircraft rather than the ninety in the Cold War. The real issue, though, is that with both the flat-tops themselves and the fast jets that go on them, the rate at which new platforms have been ordered is insufficient to sustain the current force. Like the US Air Force, the US Navy's fighter force is ageing and at present there are only plans to buy 240 new F-35C jets, even though hundreds of early-model F/A-18s are nearing the end of their lives. As for the reduced number of escorts available to protect the carriers: if the ship is cruising in the Gulf, sending bombing missions to Afghanistan or Iraq, that set-up is perfectly good. But if the US Navy had to prepare for battle against

China or Russia it would have to protect the flat-top against the full gamut of threats, from air strike to submarine, mine or cruise-missile attack, and large, Cold War-style escort groups would be back in fashion. As the cuts currently planned go ahead that will become much harder to achieve, and this too will limit the US Navy. For within the force of a 240-ship fleet, there might be sixty or so submarines and twenty or twenty-five amphibious warfare ships, leaving a surface fleet of around 155 to 160 vessels, including carriers. The numbers still seem large, but they have to be measured against the fleet at its six-hundred-ship high tide of the 1980s, that global multi-ocean missions will always force numerous sub-divisions of American naval power, and against the fact that the forces which might be arrayed against them have expanded exponentially in some parts of the world.

China has invested large amounts in the weapons and tactics to counter, or in extremis sink, American flat-tops if it had to. What's more, China plans to have two or three carriers of its own by 2030. When one looks at other aspects of naval power, such as mine warfare, shore-based cruise missiles or aviation, and small diesel-electric submarines, it is clear that several countries have either developed or are well on their way to developing the means to shut out the US Navy, or to cause it very severe difficulties, if it attempted to enter their part of the world.

Of course the obsession with carriers as totems of American superiority ignores the many indices of military power in which they are not top dogs. Other countries have long had the edge in manpower or number of tanks, or indeed in nuclear weapons: the USSR, then Russian, stockpile remains larger than that of the US. It's also true that the US, being a nation separated from its potential enemies by oceans, has long made a huge investment in its navy, whereas in Russia or China the army takes the prime role.

The one area where the United States retains an unarguable superiority and is likely to do so for decades is that of technical intelligence gathering. The disclosures of Edward Snowden underscored the vast size of this bureaucracy and its formidable reach, particularly across the internet. While tank fleets or fighter jets might be old metrics of power, there can be little doubt of the vast effort being made by the US and its English-speaking colleagues in the signals intelligence business to 'master the internet', in the words of one of the documents leaked by Snowden. The US and its partners (principally the UK's GCHQ, as well as Australian, Canadian and New Zealand agencies) have gone to great lengths to tap the fibre-optic trunks and switching centres required to gain broad global access to the net. The 'black budget' that emerged from the same tide of revelations showed the US intelligence community to be spending $52.6 billion in 2013 and employing some 107,000 people.

There are some caveats, though, in assessing the powerful web of surveillance created by the US. In the first place, much of the gathering of phone or internet data has been aimed at protecting the US and its allies from terrorist attack – i.e., it is defensive in nature against what might previously have been characterised as a law-enforcement target. Secondly, the spying against foreign governments, including allied ones, may have produced reams of data, but it has hardly given the White House magic answers to foreign policy dilemmas or arrested its decline as an economy or military power.

The budgetary cuts stem, of course, from the wider economic picture and political gridlock in Washington leading to 'sequestration' or mandatory spending cuts, which in itself is a product of the as yet unsuccessful attempts to cut the federal deficit. The political reasons for cutting US military spending from 3.9 per cent to 2.9 per cent of GDP in a few years were given by the Obama administration as an attempt to use more 'smart power' and to shift the world towards a foreign policy based on principles of common humanity. In the summer of 2014, with crises ablaze across the Middle East, Russian troops fighting in Ukraine and growing tension between China and its neighbours, Mitt Romney took to the op-ed pages of the *Washington Post* to urge the president and country to re-think the planned cuts. Brushing aside the fact that US defence spending still outranks that of its closest rivals by a wide margin, Romney wrote, 'Russia and China don't report their actual defense spending, they pay their servicemen a tiny fraction of what we pay ours and their cost to build military armament is also a fraction of ours.' Ultimately, he concluded, the Obama administration was cutting its defences in order to maintain social benefits at home, and he urged Congress to halt the process because 'freedom and peace are in the balance'.

Romney's call may prove a little less futile than his 2012 presidential campaign. The cuts continue, although in early 2015, following poor results for the Democratic Party in the mid-term elections, the White House did propose cutting by a little less, or restoring some funds to the Pentagon. At the same time, though, new imperatives, such as securing the nuclear-weapon stockpile, investing in a new strategic bomber, and finding the funds to buy more than one of the new *Gerald R. Ford*-class aircraft carriers, are appearing far faster than any small budgetary relief could fund. So despite some tinkering with the budget by almost all measurements of conventional or hard power America's clout is still reducing. 'If the US is unwilling or less able to serve as a global security provider, the world will be less stable,' writes Mathew Burrows, formerly one of the top US intelligence analysts, in his book *The Future, Declassified*. He also notes

that, 'The international system becomes more frag-
mented and deterrence against going to war begins to
weaken.'

Opinions appear to be divided among America's
service chiefs as to whether their forces have already
become 'hollow' – i.e., a good deal less capable than
they might appear – due to a sustained lack of investment in high-end warfare. While some people argue
that these chiefs have an obvious budgetary interest in
giving dire warnings, I've heard other defence leaders
say privately that they hesitate to describe publicly
how low certain US military capabilities have fallen for
fear of encouraging the country's enemies or undermining their own people. Admiral Bill Fallon cautions
against using the term 'hollow', since he feels it paints
too gloomy a picture of US readiness as well as morale.
But after a decade of underinvestment in conventional
war-fighting he concedes that 'in the US Navy the
level of readiness that you'd like to see is not there'.

What seems clearer is that many in Europe, the
Middle East and Asia have not yet registered how old
much of the United States military's equipment has
become, how far its numbers have already fallen, and

how projected cuts will make it impossible for America to have the kind of military reach it used to. The loss in numbers of fighters or warships will be marked during the next ten years, and this draw-down is now inevitable because of the block obsolescence of much of the Pentagon's equipment and the last decade's lack of investment in follow-on systems. And yet, because of this lag in perceptions, many still regard the US as somehow responsible for myriad security crises around the world and are ready either to castigate it for inaction or for taking steps that are not deemed sufficiently effective.

For many – perhaps most – American voters, economies at the Pentagon take second place to the daily challenge of earning a living in a globalised economy. The US still deploys big armed forces, after all. But in my view, many Americans do not realise that the age of a single global hyperpower is over. And, actually, it's worse than that. For it is only by combining metrics of that decline with the growth in military capabilities elsewhere that you can gain a sense of how quickly the scales are tipping.

5

The Multi-Polar World

Early on during the Ukraine crisis, in March 2014, viewers of Russia's Channel One TV news were treated to an on-screen polemic by its director Dmitry Kiselyov. He urged caution on the West in its response to what was happening in Crimea and noted that 'Russia is the only country in the world able to turn the USA into radioactive ashes.' This nuclear sabre-rattling from a man regarded as particularly close to the Kremlin came during a season of editorial bombast from Russian state-controlled media in which the interim government in Kiev was frequently described as fascist or even

Nazi, and the population was led to believe that standing in the way of Moscow's attempts to defend Russian-speakers could be tantamount to risking a third world war.

Although I was well aware of these messages, I was taken aback when visiting Moscow two months later to see a report several minutes long concerning 'military exercises' leading the same Channel One evening bulletin. It showed salvoes of rockets being fired, tanks advancing and President Putin taking charge of it all from an underground war room before ordering the launch of an intercontinental ballistic missile. This choreographed display of might had a feel of North Korean war hysteria about it. It brought home how fundamentally different the role of Russian media had become in trying to shape public opinion and condition it to the use of force. In the first instance, in the UK or US it would be quite inconceivable for a report about military manoeuvres (rather than actual combat operations) to lead a national news bulletin, and to do so at such length. Furthermore, it pressed home Kiselyov's earlier message that Russia was prepared to brandish its nuclear arsenal in order to get what it wanted. The idea of an American president reminding the world of the nuclear weapons at his disposal in a speech on al-Qaeda, or indeed Ukraine, is so inconceivable as to suggest fundamental underlying differences.

The idea that Mr Kiselyov was just a commentator, free to express his views in the way that extremists might do on Western TV, might have taken in some people. But he soon found himself under a European Union travel ban and asset freeze for acting as the Kremlin's primary mouthpiece in justifying its actions in Ukraine. And President Putin himself used similar language: in August 2014, for example, when he told other countries 'it's best not to mess with us' over Ukraine and reminded them that his country was a considerable nuclear power. This type of utterance, combined with his public statements following the annexation of Crimea, caused deep alarm in many Western capitals for they appeared to announce a doctrine of going to the aid of Russian-speaking communities, with troops if necessary, across internationally recognised borders. These events violated a principle enshrined in the UN Charter, and often eloquently defended by the Kremlin itself, that territorial disputes (such as that in Crimea) should never be settled by force.

In his speech on the annexation of Crimea, Putin referred back to the collapse of the Soviet Union, an event he had previously described as one of the greatest disasters of the twentieth century. 'Millions of people went to bed in one country and awoke in different ones,' noted the Russian president, 'overnight becoming ethnic minorities in former Union republics, while the Russian nation became one of the biggest, if not the biggest ethnic group in the world to be divided by borders.'

This seemed to open up the prospect not just of trouble in Ukraine but in countries like Kazakhstan or the Baltic Republics, where there are large Russian populations. In the latter case, since Estonia, Latvia and Lithuania had joined the Nato alliance it raised the prospect of renewed confrontation between East and West, or indeed actual conflict if the Kremlin moved against them.

This change proved so alarming to some observers that they posited Putin would stop at nothing to achieve his aims, and that the nuclear threats were there not just to convince Nato to stay out of Ukraine but ultimately, if necessary, to convince the Americans not to fight on Europe's behalf.

'In a more volatile geopolitical situation,' wrote the dissident Russian commentator Andrey Piontkovsky, 'a nuclear power focused on changing the existing status quo, enjoying the advantage of political will and indifferent to the values of human lives (its own and others), and affected by a certain adventurism, could achieve serious foreign policy results by the threat of the application or the limited application of nuclear weapons.' His article, while certainly not inspired by the Kremlin, was accepted by many experts in Moscow as an accurate reflection of Mr Putin's new strategic thinking.

As for the possibility of actually using weapons of mass destruction, Piontkovsky put forward a scenario in which Russia moved against one of the Baltic republics, triggering an attempt to help them from other Nato allies. 'Putin knows that they know that if they come to the assistance of Estonia, then Putin can respond with a very limited nuclear strike and destroy for example two European capitals. Not London and not Paris, of course.' The idea that such a use of nuclear strikes to 'de-couple', in Cold War parlance, the US from its European allies has received some further credence with the leaking of suggestions that Russian strategic forces exercises in 2009 and 2013 involved hitting Warsaw.

Leaving aside such apocalyptic analyses, there can be little doubt that, following the entry of Russian regular troops into eastern Ukraine in August 2014, few Western leaders harboured any illusions that Russia had the will to use its armed forces to re-draw the map and that it was also reaping the dividends of a long reinvestment in these capabilities. For as the armed forces of European countries or the US have been dwindling over the past decade, those of Russia have been reconstituted following the post-Soviet collapse and are now receiving substantial investment.

The Soviet legacy gives Russia certain areas of military power in which it is unmatched – their equivalent of America's carrier groups or spy satellites. Being a continental power with hugely long borders, Russia has always maintained a big army, though in the

1990s it did effectively collapse after the fall of the USSR. Its air defence, established as a separate service, has a national network of radar, surface-to-air missiles and fighters unmatched anywhere in the world. Speaking in September 2014, General Philip Breedlove, Nato's Supreme Commander (and an air force officer by trade), conceded that this system was so formidable that 'if we ever had to go into that and fight, we're going to have to address it'. During the fighting in eastern Ukraine the separatists were taken under the umbrella of Russian air defence, with the consequence that in a few months two dozen Ukrainian planes and helicopters had been shot down over their own country. This was achieved in part by deploying advanced surface-to-air missile systems like the Buk (a type of weapon of which the UK and many other European armed forces actually have no equivalent) into eastern Ukraine, with the terrible consequence that a Malaysian Airlines Boeing 777, Flight MH-17, was shot down with the loss of all 298 people on board.

Not content with its current capabilities, Russia continues to invest heavily in its air defences. As a part of this, it is upgrading the Moscow anti-ballistic missile network, the world's only operational shield against strategic nuclear weapons. It has started testing new A-135 interceptor missiles. Recent investments in low-frequency upgrades for its radar network have led some analysts to conclude that Russia has cracked the problem of detecting stealth aircraft, which, if true, could nullify Nato's vast investment in the F-35 before it has even been declared operational. What is so impressive about the Russian air defence is that it represents a big investment in the capabilities required for state-on-state warfare. As General Breedlove intimated, even the US has largely given up the business of assuring it can penetrate such defences, and instead its major spending in the past decade has been on capabilities such as intelligence, surveillance platforms or drones to kill outlaws with Kalashnikovs.

Today Russia is not only the world's largest nuclear-weapon state (in terms of warheads deployed), but it is also the one with the greatest capability to defend against air or missile attacks on its soil by another state. It is also embarking on big defence-spending increases to modernise its conventional forces. Current plans envisage a 44 per cent increase in defence spending over three years. Of course it can be argued that such an investment is needed, since many of Russia's combat aircraft and warships are even older than America's. So scores of new fighter planes are on order, along with drones, tanks, warships and all manner of other destructive *matériel*. The Airborne Forces, which featured prominently in the seizure of Crimea, are due to double in size, to seventy-two thousand troops, by 2019.

Russia's planned spending increases may well prove unaffordable, for the economy was already grinding to a halt before the Western sanctions imposed in 2014 caused it to totter. The plunging oil price is an even bigger headache for the Kremlin, and some argue the fall in revenues from hydrocarbons threatens even President Putin's position. But even if his planned military build-up cannot now be funded, Russia has already taken its forces to the point where it is the global leader in several areas. Equally important, given the need of any aspiring military power to match capability with intent, the Kremlin has shown the willingness to use them.

America's other principal strategic rival, by way of contrast, has shown itself to be far more cautious. For much of the past decade, 'declinists' in the US have been obsessed with China. The mainspring of US–Chinese rivalry has been trade rather than hard power. As Chinese enterprises have hoovered up man-ufacturing contracts, minerals and markets, they have caught up with the US. Current estimates suggest China will have the world's largest economy by 2025.

As its economy swells it has been easy for China to finance larger defence budgets. It has sought to match or nullify many areas of US technological superiority, with major efforts in its space programme, cyber war-fare, stealth aircraft, guided missiles and blue-water fleet. In all these cases China takes a very long view, understanding that it may be decades before it can match American sophistication. In some, though, such as cyber warfare and guided missiles, they are already advanced and able to pose a serious threat to Western networks and ships respectively.

The principal points of difference between China's leadership and that of Russia are that it has retained a more collective character, and that the senior leadership of the Chinese Communist Party has shown itself to be more cautious, primarily concerned with achieving economic rather than strategic hegemony, and it thinks in terms of decades. For years Deng Xiaoping's 1990 dictum, 'we should keep a low profile and bide our time', dominated foreign policy thinking in Beijing. However, the way China deploys its power has changed and has done so in part due to a groundswell of nationalist sentiment. Popular hatred of Japan in particular is so strong that a dispute over uninhabited islands (known as the Senkaku group to the Japanese and Diaoyu to China) has triggered sabre-rattling and attempts by China to extend its airspace over the area. Games of nerve with coast guard vessels or fighter planes manoeuvring in close proximity (and sometimes colliding) have become a frequent part of this new tension – so much so that prior to Russia's action in Ukraine many strategic analysts were predicting that Japan and China were the two countries in the world most likely to go to war.

It's not just about an old resentment of Japan. In the South China Sea, a growing naval presence and Beijing's championing of the rights of ethnic Chinese have worried neighbours that are home to such populations. US planes are also getting buzzed by Chinese fighters. The growing use of a 1947 map compounds the alarm of countries like Vietnam, Taiwan and the Philippines, since it rules part of their territory into Chinese space.

This change in regional mood has become particularly notable since 2012 and the appointment of Xi Jinping as president. China may have been thinking very long-term, but it has evidently recalculated on the basis that it is rising faster than expected and America declining likewise. So in 2005, for example, a Chinese analyst suggested that it would be 2050 'before it can be called a modernised, medium-level developed country', yet even the recent Western calculation cited above predicts that the Chinese economy will become the world's largest a quarter of a century sooner than this.

Those familiar with Chinese technological espionage efforts argue that it has played a key role in catching up. 'There's been pretty much unrestricted Chinese aggression in the economic space to close the gap much more quickly than they would have done otherwise,' Admiral Bill Fallon, himself a former Pacific fleet commander, told me.

By 2013, at a meeting with Barack Obama at the Sunnylands ranch in California, President Xi said they were striving for 'a new model of great power relations'. Far from some sort of middling status, China was announcing, through this and numerous other pronouncements, that it had become one of the big boys. Although many of America's traditional allies were nervous about even tacit acceptance of this new Chinese language, Secretary of State John Kerry did precisely that in August 2014 when he said the US and China were 'busy trying to define a new great power relationship'.

There are still many, on both sides of the Pacific, who believe a new Cold War-style Sino-American rift can be avoided. Mathew Burrows heard from such optimists when he was in China talking to the policy elite. But he heard other views too, including an official who told him 'it is a foregone conclusion that there will be a showdown between China and the United States, not necessarily militarily, but one side will enforce its will on the other side'.

This view finds its echo in America. Rational officials in the Pentagon or CIA are hardly clamouring for war with China; far from it. But they see in the increasingly vexed rivalry between the countries all manner of scope for future conflict. Handling this, in the view of many such players, is the USA's principal foreign policy and strategic challenge for the coming century. 'The biggest issue for the US long term is not so much in the military system,' says Admiral Fallon, 'but as to how we change their political system without regime change.'

Some of China's neighbours, particularly Japan, have drawn their own conclusions about the geopolitical trend and are busy boosting their military preparations. But while the US's ability to project power close to China has declined significantly in recent years, and is set to do so still further, countries like Japan, Malaysia and the Philippines have defence treaties with America that could easily be invoked in an emergency.

So, just as President Putin's implied threats against the Baltic republics are now setting some Western strategic planners squirming, because of the obligations of Nato membership, so there are equivalent scenarios being played out in the Far East. In the case of Japan, President Obama has explicitly reiterated the US's commitment to its security and strengthened its hand in the Senkaku dispute, for example, by flying US Air Force planes through China's self-declared airspace control zone over the islands. But if China flexed its muscles with Vietnam or Taiwan in some future crisis, could it play out much like Ukraine?

For many in the West there is still a reluctance to think Russia or China might provoke a direct military confrontation, and it is the emergence of powerful non-state groups – particularly the Islamic State group in Iraq and Syria – that poses the biggest immediate risk to their security. This might seem to be little more than a continuation, albeit revved up, of the long-running Sunni insurgency in western Iraq and Syria. However, the availability of large amounts of cash from oil sales, the ability to attract thousands of foreign volunteers, and weaponry from captured garrisons has put ISIS into a higher threat category than almost any other non-state group. It has picked up man-portable anti-aircraft systems, armour and mustard gas. The group operates drones, an intelligence network and sophisticated information operations.

'I believe that extreme non-state organisations like ISIS are more of a threat to our way of life than Russia and China,' General Lord Richards, Chief of the Defence Staff until 2014, told me, 'because the former recognise no norms of accepted behaviour and yearn to destroy our way of life. They can also attack from within.'

If there is one non-state group that outdoes the Islamic State in terms of military capability, it is Lebanon's Shia movement, Hezbollah. It has large numbers of long-range rockets, as well as other sophisticated weapons, and a huge amount of combat experience. Hezbollah also showed itself resilient to a lengthy pounding from the Israelis in 2006. But whereas Hezbollah has involved itself in the Syrian war, placing itself squarely against Sunni militancy, it has not resorted to ideology as extreme as ISIS, nor acted in the same way, such as by murdering hundreds of prisoners or implying that it rejects any restraint on its use of force.

A third non-state group merits a mention here:

Boko Haram in Nigeria. While having some superficial similarity with ISIS and Hezbollah, being a militant Islamic organisation (its name translates as 'Western teaching is unclean') there are some significant differences. It shares the Islamic State's willingness to use extreme violence, but barely feels the need to justify its acts, even to its own support base. Boko Haram is also operating across borders. Unchecked, it threatens not just the stability of Nigeria but of central and west Africa more widely.

Of the other emerging state powers, and big spenders on defence – India, Saudi Arabia or the United Arab Emirates – less need be said in that they have been strategic partners of the US for decades. It is worth noting, though, that they are pushing middle-ranking players like the UK and France down the hard power league table.

In 2014, the International Institute for Strategic Studies assessed that Saudi Arabia had become the world's fourth-largest defence spender (after the USA, Russia and China), relegating the UK to fifth. The new Indian government of Narendra Modi has committed itself to a 12 per cent budgetary increase, and to knock Saudi Arabia out of fourth place by 2020.

India's ambitions for its military and defence industry are in many ways enormous. Its naval shipbuilding programme aims to produce a two-hundred-ship fleet, including three aircraft carriers, by 2025. It is developing its own spy satellites, nuclear submarines (including ones carrying ballistic missiles) and, as a partner with Russia, stealth aircraft. Increasingly, the Indian government perceives itself to be China's geopolitical rival as the two countries jostle for friends in a region extending east from the Arabian Peninsula, through the Indian Ocean and Strait of Malacca to the South China Sea. Nobody thinks India is intent on military confrontation with China, but it is becoming such a significant power that it could either combine very effectively with the US against that country or, alternatively, block the Americans in its own backyard.

Underlying all calculations of the growing power of countries like China or India is the fact that they are nuclear weapons states. Back in the 1970s, the US could have threatened either with a beating by conventional forces, leaving the smaller country with the choice of whether to threaten nuclear escalation, a course of action that was not credible because they had little ability to hit the US homeland, whereas American nuclear strikes would have proven ruinous to them. Now these countries, and of course Russia, have sufficiently strong conventional forces that they could defend themselves that way, and the US would be left with the choice of nuclear escalation or backing down.

This is the cold, hard truth behind growing talk of global multi-polarity and the ability of these other players to create their own spheres of influence. Of course there are other nuclear weapon states, such as Israel and Pakistan, where the threat of nuclear oblivion conditions the behaviour of some neighbours, rather than the US or West more generally.

It is hardly surprising given all this that Iraq, Syria, North Korea and Iran should have tried to acquire nuclear weapons in recent decades. Under Saddam Hussein, Iraq also built up enormous conventional forces. The destruction of these in 1991 required the US to deploy more than half a million personnel, six carrier groups and eleven divisions of ground forces, and to fly 116,000 air missions.

The US armed forces would today be incapable of mounting an operation of similar size. Even a conventional military campaign against Iran could prove a real challenge. The same could be said of North Korea, with its outmoded but vast conventional forces and small nuclear capability. Against a full-scale invasion of South Korea, the US would have little choice but to go nuclear.

In this situation, some countries that have invested enormously in conventional defence and have grown nervous as to whether they can depend on American help will inevitably keep asking themselves the nuclear weapon question. So far the Saudis in particular have couched the question in terms of a determination to deploy such devices if Iran does. There is considerable evidence that Saudi Arabia has agreements with Pakistan to supply the bombs, and that such devices may indeed sit ready for shipment in that country. In the longer term, though, and particularly if diplomacy fails to resolve the Iranian question, both Saudi Arabia and the UAE may well develop home-grown atomic weapons.

As countries acquire nuclear weapons they do not

necessarily buy complete immunity from Western military action, but they do move into a category in which a major confrontation would be possible only in the most extreme circumstances of national survival. Russia, China, India, Israel, Pakistan and North Korea might already be said to have moved into that category. But now these and some other countries could also mount a credible conventional defence that would leave the United States having to think the unthinkable, with profound implications for the world.

6

The Vanishing Consensus

The 2014 United Nations General Assembly in New York provided a fine example of a new type of realpolitik in action, and with it the evaporation of principle in international politics. The leaders of 140 countries criss-crossed the city, doing their business in countless 'bi-laterals' on the fringes of the formal event. There were more police escorts, guntoting special agents and bag-carriers attending the potentates than ever before. And the gap between the ideals of the UN and the actual behaviour of its members had never seemed wider.

The US president sat down for meetings with an Egyptian president who had overthrown his elected predecessor; an Indian prime minister who for years had been denied an American visa for allegedly inciting Hindu extremism; and a Turkish president who was asked to help fight the militancy in Syria that he had done much to foster. Of course, it could equally be said, as the US marshalled a coalition to bomb those extremists of the self-proclaimed Islamic State, that it was also failing to act in the spirit of the UN's founding charter, which proposed collective solutions in the face of serious threats to international security. Instead, having done nothing for years while civil war ravaged Syria and destabilised the region, Mr Obama was acting in response to domestic political outrage following the beheading of two American journalists.

The UN Charter of 1945 is a key document in defining how nations, together, should try to keep the peace, and indeed use force legitimately. It does permit nations to wage war on one another – but only in self-defence. It forbids interference in the internal affairs of other countries, although more recently adopted amendments allow for that if to prevent genocide.

Central to the order that the charter's creators tried to perpetuate was the idea of major powers combining to deal with the world's big problems, as they had just done with Nazi Germany and Japan. This was enshrined in the arrangements for the Security Council, a fifteen-member body empowered to deal with serious threats to international security and to do so in a way binding on all UN members. Five of the Security Council's members – the US, UK, France, Russia and China – were given permanent member-ship and veto powers; the rest are elected from the organisation's wider membership.

It is true to say that the post-1945 consensus about war and peace has always been elusive. Many Westerners overestimate the degree to which the UN or indeed international law more widely has been able to regulate conflict. Indeed, the imprimatur of a fully-fledged, enabling Security Council resolution has only ever been given to three wars: Korea in 1950; the attack on Saddam Hussein's Iraq in 1991; and the Nato operation to bomb Libya in 2011.

For decades, it was the Cold War that deadlocked the Security Council. After the USSR had, farcically, boycotted the meeting that voted through the Korean War resolution, Moscow learned the value of the veto. As did the US. With the fall of the Berlin Wall this impasse was broken, and after the vote for a war to reverse Saddam's aggression against Kuwait some proclaimed a new world order had arrived.

Nato's success in the Cold War produced some short-lived triumphalism. Francis Fukuyama famously wrote of the 'end of history' and the triumph of Western democratic values. The Warsaw Pact was dissolved and its members queued up to join Nato – some seeing membership of the organisation as a waypoint to the European Union and a future integrated with the Western economy. After the collapse of the Soviet Union some of its former republics even sought the same package. Estonia, Latvia and Lithuania eventually made it, while other countries that saw themselves embracing the Western future, such as Georgia and Ukraine, were left stranded.

Having spent a good deal of time in Russia between 1990 and 1994, I well remember that many people there welcomed the change wholeheartedly, espousing Western political values and, if they had the money, indulging in an orgy of consumerism. Although the Kremlin has subsequently painted the expansion of Nato and the EU as an ill-starred encroachment in a traditionally Russian space, such ideas disappeared, for a time at least, from mainstream discourse after the reunification of Germany (which Mikhail Gorbachev had objected to) and the dissolution of the USSR. When one heard Russian objections to the Western embrace of erstwhile allies or indeed actual Soviet republics being raised back then, they came from extreme nationalists or communists. Evidently, though, this narrative tapped into deeper public fears and fed on a sense of humiliation felt by many Russians, even if the likes of Boris Yeltsin and his government absolutely and explicitly accepted the changes in Eastern Europe. In time, this rout of the old Soviet system, and the deals done in the 1990s to bring one-time allies into the Western orbit, would provide plenty of fuel for those seeking to restore Russian national pride. Almost all of the former military and intelligence chiefs I have spoken to believe that the West, in its triumphalism, the extension of Nato and its reluctance to engage in true strategic cooperation with the Kremlin, committed major errors during the 1990s.

What's more, the overwhelming of Iraq, a considerable military power at the time, temporarily created what some called a 'mono-polar' world in which the USA had become a 'hyper-power' whose might had to be constrained. And this provided Russia, and China in particular, with a rationale for new vetoes. But something else was going on too, even a few years after the Gulf War. Russia started referring to an idea much deeper in its history as it stood in the way of Western attempts to intervene in the Yugoslav civil war: the principle of solidarity with fellow Slavs. With the removal of the glacial grip of superpower deadlock the politics of identity – religious and national – began a powerful resurgence in many parts of the world. The chance of collective action, sanctioned by the Security Council, once again grew more remote. And indeed the actions of its permanent members, the US and UK in Iraq or Russia in Georgia and Ukraine, further undermined the chances of global consensus.

Underlying all of this difficulty in achieving common views is the re-emergence of nationalist or religious ideas harmful to cooperation. Increasingly, the Chinese world view is couched in Confucian terms rather than those of the Western philosophical canon. Attacks on American values, portraying them as a threat to traditional Chinese ones, have become common in state media. An article by Zhou Xiaoping called 'Nine Knockout Blows in America's Cold War against China' was widely circulated in the autumn of 2014. Blow No. 1 was 'Exterminate idols. Destroy Chinese moral models and replace them with American idols'; Blow No. 2: 'Target the long-held beliefs of Chinese civilisation, eliminate ancestor worship and replace it with the worship of Westerners and Jesus Christ', and so on. Mr Zhou was described as an 'independent blogger', and there are plenty of those worldwide espousing outlandish ideas, but the widespread syndication of the article in state-controlled outlets showed it had a measure of party endorsement and had tapped into an undercurrent of hostility to the US and its values.

Muslim scholars who seek to modernise the faith, meanwhile, struggle against interpretations that rank the rights of believers ahead of those who do not embrace Islam. Hindu nationalism has triumphed politically in India, and the Israeli government contains people who wonder aloud about driving out the

Palestinian population. As for the Russians, under President Putin they have been much more assertive about their 'traditional values', rejecting for example the acceptance of gay people in Western societies.

With governments and militant groups now in possession of their own cable channels, web pages and social media accounts, they are able to tailor their messages to specific audiences, with those intended for domestic consumption often a good deal more assertive than those intended for wider consumption. Within this discourse, Western concepts of righteous behaviour can often be discarded in favour of very different stuff. Ilya Zaslavsky of the Chatham House think tank asserts that President Putin uses 'liquid ideology', trading on cynicism about politics in a new way. 'They actually want to present Russia as a baddie and a bully,' says Zaslavsky. 'It conveniently folds into their own virtual neo-Cold War reality, where Russia is a besieged castle surrounded by enemies and has to fight back.'

Under this interpretation recent Kremlin statements, for example those mentioning nuclear weapons in the context of Ukraine, are deliberately intended to appal and frighten European countries into staying out of Russia's business, while impressing people at home with their toughness. It is a wilful rejection of the conventions of international behaviour that existed even a decade ago. Sir John Sawers, Chief of MI6 until 2014, has underscored the importance of this change, noting in the context of the Ukraine crisis that 'for now, we can't identify shared values with Russia. Our attempt to find order based on values is giving us disorder.'

A far more extreme example of this can be seen in the communiqués and social media output of the Islamic State group. It has distributed images of its fighters murdering hundreds of prisoners or beheading hostages. The aim is, in part, to terrify other opponents, and in another to impress their own public with their ruthless commitment to building the caliphate. But this is just the most extreme version of something that has become widespread – a state or group stating quite overtly, often to rally its support base, that it doesn't care what the international community thinks or what human rights groups or statutes may say. It happened in the US after 9/11, after all.

In 2015 the UN Charter and other expressions of a

one-time consensus about attaining international justice, such as the Universal Declaration of Human Rights, seem, if not entirely dead, to be little more than props in the rhetorical armoury of countries determined to behave in their own interest. Addressing the General Assembly in September 2014, Barack Obama stated explicitly: 'Russia's actions in Ukraine challenge [the] post-war order.' The Kremlin, he said, has 'a vision of the world in which might makes right – a world in which one nation's borders can be redrawn by another'.

With the decline of Western will and the capability to police conflict, it appears to be spreading in many parts of the world. Much of the Middle East is in turmoil; Nigeria, one of the biggest players in Africa, is succumbing to religious war; and there are numerous possible flashpoints around China's periphery. Stepping down from running the Pentagon's intelligence machine in the summer of 2014, Lieutenant-General Michael T. Flynn said, 'I think we're in a period of prolonged societal conflict that is pretty unprecedented.' These emergencies are also developing more quickly, he noted, because 'that change is being accelerated by the explosion of social media'.

This may look like a crisis on an immense scale in the Pentagon, but of course to many around the world it is a great big opportunity. That was how President Putin saw his chance to grab Crimea, or the militant Islamic State group to sweep through northern Iraq. And this kind of action, whether moderated through social media or the ballot box, can be extremely popular.

President Putin's approval rating soared to over 80 per cent due to his handling of the Ukraine crisis. When Israel struck Gaza, killing two thousand people, mostly civilians, one poll showed that only 4 per cent of Jewish Israelis felt this was excessive force. Were China to sink a Japanese ship off the islands disputed between them, doubtless it would be very popular in that country too.

In much of the world the idea that political power grows from the barrel of a gun is – if it ever went away – now back with a vengeance. And of course it is recognition of this that lies behind the substantial increases in defence spending by Russia, India, the Gulf States and a good many others.

Apart from some expressions of alarm or compassion

for those caught up in conflicts, these trends do not seem to be worrying Western leaders unduly. Or they are simply choosing to ignore them, because they are terrified of the possible consequences. So, for example, Nato members committed in September 2014 to achieve a budgetary target (2 per cent of GDP on the military by 2024) while many, including such powerful players as France and Germany, continued to pare away below that. As for the USA, its president recognises the gravity of threats to the post-1945 global order, yet presses on with deep cuts to the military. The cumulative effects of American cuts and others' increases is shown by the fact that the Pentagon's share of global defence spending has fallen from 47 per cent in 2010 to 38 per cent in 2014.

The Russian author and Kremlin critic Mikhail Shishkin argues that 'Putin knows that the West cannot cross the red line that he himself has long crossed and left behind. The red line is the willingness to go to war.' Shishkin does not call Europe's attitude 'appeasement', as some in the West do. Rather, he explains it in terms of denial, writing, 'Europeans are not ready for the new reality that has set in. Leave us alone! Return everything to the way it was: jobs, gas, peace!'

Those who would dispute Shishkin's thesis might point to the use of economic sanctions against Russia as a consequence of its behaviour. If the West uses such measures these days instead of military confrontation, that must be infinitely preferable. The argument about whether sanctions can actually change Putin's mind is ongoing. But the acknowledgement that Western countries are engaging in state-versus-state coercion using economic pressure points is in itself an important metric of how different today's situation is from those heady years after the collapse of the Soviet Union. And indeed, even if the Kremlin's current woes were to topple Putin, it would be naive to assume that most Russians would either change their attitude to Ukraine or be anything other than resentful about the Western role in strongarming their country.

Shishkin and some other Russian pessimists argue that sanctions are in fact helpful to the Kremlin because they allow Putin to propagate a war mentality by requiring people to suffer hardship. Hence he points to the Russian counter-sanctions of banning certain Western agricultural products as designed to harm not just the exporters but Putin's own people, spurring a resentment of the outside world.

I'm not sure I share Shishkin's view on that particular, and reckon that Putin has responded to the imposition of sanctions or threat of further ones by scaling back activities in Ukraine at certain times. But it can be argued that these were simply tactical gambits rather than a change to his strategic objective of dominating Ukraine.

While the Kremlin would obviously dispute much of Shishkin's analysis, its response to sanctions and other Western counter-measures resulting from the Ukraine situation has often been uncompromising. In a key policy speech in October 2014, Sergey Lavrov, the Russian Foreign Minister, noted that relations with the US had sunk to a very low level due to Washington's 'attempts at restoring the mono-polar world'. Signalling that this new reality was here to stay, and that the White House had better get used to it, he noted, 'Americans need time to reappraise their place in the world in general, to understand the developments of the past decade, realise that there is no alternative to the further strengthening of the multi-polar trend.'

Interestingly, the Kremlin has responded to these sanctions by deepening trading relations with countries like China and Iran. In that speech, Lavrov specifically noted the growing role of the G20, the Shanghai Cooperation Organisation (the club of Russia, China and four Central Asian states founded in 1996), and the BRIC grouping. As for Iran, the Islamic Republic was itself subjected to the Western sanctions' 'nuclear option' of suspension from SWIFT, the international banking transaction system. Many credited this with bringing Iran to the negotiating table in 2013, and some argue it should now be used against Russia. In an attempt to get ahead of such threats, Russian officials are now talking about leaving that system in 2015 anyway.

Sanctions have not stopped the pursuit by these countries of what they regard as their basic natural rights, and probably cannot do so. In Iran's case, this is about maintaining control of its nuclear programme, including the ability to enrich uranium, and in Russia's the question of bringing Russian-speakers in neighbouring republics back into the mother country.

Long term, the use of the economic weapon as an

alternative to war may be self-defeating. By encouraging the emergence of a non-Western bloc of nations (which could easily include Russia, China and Iran, among others) with a complex bi-lateral web of trade deals and ultimately, in the long term, even its own reserve currency (China's) it may reduce interdependence with the West. With their reliance on Western capital and markets thus lessened, that could be the starting point for even greater readiness to use force.

To add to the confusion in Western societies, many do not consider their nations reluctant to wage war. This stems from a belief that selective military action against some of the symptoms of growing global disorder, such as air strikes against Islamic militants, involves state killing and is therefore 'war'. Well, it may be, but only in the sense that buying a chocolate bar or a private jet can both be called shopping. Campaigns such as those against the Islamic State or Somali pirates involve taking life on the scale of industrial accidents, and below that of road traffic smashes. This type of action is not, critically, a struggle between two or more societies in which a nation is mobilised and asked to make sacrifices. Those countries that plan seriously for war between states, from Russia to China or Israel, almost all have national service. Western countries have largely abolished it. As for their priorities in spending national resources, I won't repeat myself.

These, then, are quite good metrics for the vanished consensus about the world and how to keep it peaceful. The politics of aspiration and legality are on one side. And, on the other, conscription, rising military spending and growing adventurism. Nationalism, and a belief in the superiority of one's own kind, can actually be found on both sides of this divide. But Western societies are no longer prepared to force the point against other states. While American neo-cons saw the invasion of Iraq as part of a scheme to export Western democracy to the Middle East, that view never gained widespread support among the American public, who tended to believe that the war was payback for 9/11 despite the lack of any substantial evidence to tie Saddam's Iraq to that act.

So by the time of the 2014 UN General Assembly, the president was no longer talking about the global march of democracy. Instead, he was rolling out the red carpet for all manner of despots, making deals with the Saudis and Turks, and trying to do one with Iran. Of course, the American or British public still think they know what ought to be done in this country or that, or at least there might be a strong majority of them in polls on an issue. Increasingly, though, people in other cultures know their view of global issues and don't intend to be dictated to. Fewer world leaders are graduates of European universities than in the days in which the UN Charter was written, and instead they answer to public opinion revved up by state-controlled and social media. They have their own ideas about war and peace now, and the Western paradigm is looking less and less relevant.

7

Back to the Jungle

What will the new world order, or lack of it, look like? In fact, we are already living through it. The US and its allies are engaged in sporadic military action against the Islamic State with little indication, so far, of success. Russia's actions in Georgia in 2008 or Ukraine in 2014 show us that the old post-war consensus about refraining from violence or respecting the borders left when the USSR collapsed has ended. Of late, we've seen China behaving in a more assertive manner too, also revisiting territorial questions and claiming great swathes of ocean and territory. Accompanying this shift, Vladimir Putin and Xi Jinping have started to use a new language, one of their rights as great powers, and their responsibilities in terms of looking after their own kind scattered about the 'near abroad'.

'The business of multi-polarity is very real now,' says Admiral Bill Fallon. 'We had our chance in the 1990s and we blew it. It is going to be a multi-polar world again, we are not going to be the only superpower.' In some respects, this is already very real. In other regions, technologies or military capabilities, the West retains a tenuous edge.

Many countries are drawing fearful conclusions from this. But the uncomfortable realities are already being digested in Estonia or Kazakhstan, Vietnam and the Philippines. It has long been apparent – for example since the USSR's invasion of Afghanistan in 1979 – that the pressure which can be brought to bear on a major nuclear weapons power invading its neighbour is distinctly limited. What is new is the explicit challenge by Russia and China to the existing order, and the apparent unwillingness of the West to answer it. The speed with which the US and Europe have sought to de-escalate tensions with the Kremlin, freezing in its gains in Crimea and eastern Ukraine, can leave little doubt in the minds of other former Soviet republics that, despite some residual sanctions in Russia and pledges of an improved Nato response, there is little willingness to risk a major war. Nineteenth-century concepts of spheres of influence have returned, along with the tendency of many Westerners to conclude that 'it's not our problem'. The emergence of a militant Islamist movement that rejects old borders in the Middle East and now has access to large amounts of money and weaponry also feels more like the 1880s than the 1980s, as it is reminiscent of the Mahdist state in Sudan back in the late nineteenth century.

For people living on one of the world's political fault lines, it has become unwise to assume that the 'international community' will ride to their rescue. This extends more widely than just the neighbours of Russia and China. It applies to many Middle Eastern countries, surveying the Shia/Sunni schism, or South Koreans looking north. Lesser but still significant chances of inter-state conflict breaking out apply in

South Asia, Africa and Latin America. For many countries, fragmentation or insurgency undermines their ability to respond to such challenges, and malign neighbours are exploiting precisely these forces to sap them by steps short of war.

If the law of the jungle now applies, many will conclude that only the fittest will survive or be able to protect their interests from predators. Late in 2014, President Putin addressed the annual meeting of the Valdai Discussion Club in a session called 'New Rules, or a Game without Rules'. Referring to this title, he said, 'I think that this formula accurately describes the historic turning point we have reached today and the choice we all face.' While Mr Putin would of course dispute his own country's role in bringing about this growing turmoil, or indeed the idea that the US has become more reluctant to intervene militarily, his diagnosis of a growing threat to global order was not so different from those of many others worldwide. This lies behind the huge spending spree on weapons going on in the Gulf and South East Asia. Ultimately, it will also lead more countries to acquire their own nuclear weapons, as well as other capabilities such as chemical, biological or cyber weaponry. Some non-state groups are also now seeking the ability to hit Western countries harder than ever before.

'In the near term,' General Stan McChrystal told me, 'cyber and/or WMD attacks offer a serious threat to our economy.' Down range, he can also see potential difficulties for US forces resulting from the tilting of world military power. 'Over a longer time span,' he argues, 'access around the world could become increasingly problematic due to instability in some areas or the rise of regional powers with aggressive designs in others.'

This concern over future 'access' – i.e., being countered by a strong regional power able to shut out foreign intervention – is shared by many military commanders. When asked whether a situation will emerge in which regional powers will be able to dominate their own backyards, General Sir Peter Wall, the head of the British Army until 2014, replied, 'It will do if we remain as detached as we are at the moment. In fact, we are already there in many areas, I suspect.'

There is an element of 'back to the future' about this vision of increased resistance to a Western-defined notion of international order. And along with a return to spheres of influence that would have been familiar to Palmerston or Bismarck, it is quite likely that countries will band together in new alliances in the face of insecurity. In this sense, the fact that Saudi Arabia and India are now spending so much on defence could be a boon for the US. When the Pentagon was looking for help in bombing the Islamic State, Saudi Arabia was ready to answer that call. If, in some nightmare of future brinkmanship, the US Navy was confronting China in its southern seas, it's possible that it might get support from an Indian carrier group approaching from the Strait of Malacca. It is on this basis, of course, that America has cooperated strategically with the Gulf States and India, allowing the export of all manner of advanced weaponry and even, in the latter case, sharing nuclear or space technology.

This sub-contracting of security to allies in certain parts of the world will however involve new accommodations. The quid pro quos of emerging powers would, once again, have been all too familiar to a Victorian statesman, but sit ill in today's age of ethical foreign policy or social-media activism where a country's human rights violations can colour its whole image in Western countries. In return for their cooperation, Saudi Arabia will be saying 'Let's have less of this Arab Spring democratisation nonsense'; the UAE urging Europe to crack down on the Muslim Brotherhood; or India getting the US to delay advanced weapons deliveries to Pakistan. Egypt provides a perfect example of a country in which America has had to default back into a modern-day form of realpolitik.

Barack Obama made a 2009 speech in Egypt, at Cairo's al-Azhar University, in which he set out a new relationship between the US and the Arab world. In that speech he insisted that the US would not try to impose democracy, but that 'government of the people and by the people sets a single standard for all who would hold power'. Yet when the democratic revolution in Egypt stumbled in 2013, the US could do nothing but watch as the military overthrew an elected president. A short-lived suspension of American weapons deliveries was soon forgotten and the US looked the other way as Egypt became increasingly involved in the civil war of its neighbour Libya. By the summer of 2014, the US was declaring Egypt to be a key partner in the common struggle against the Islamic State, the new form of Islamic militancy. The success of Egypt's military takeover has thus exposed the hollowness of Western rhetoric.

Even at the height of the Cold War, the White House experienced limits to its power and sometimes found itself thwarted. Now, with global economic and, increasingly, military power being reassigned, this experience is becoming more commonplace. In this situation, some have found little difficulty embracing realpolitik. Faced with the sweeping gains of the Islamic State group, for example, Lord Ashdown advocated setting aside differences over Ukraine with Vladimir Putin in the interests of a common front against the jihadists. Former senior UK military figures such as Lord Dannatt meanwhile urged alliance with President Bashar al-Assad of Syria against the same foe. General Lord Richards, until recently Chief of the UK's Defence Staff, believes China and Russia must be engaged in the larger strategic interest of stopping ISIS from re-making the Middle East. 'China's rise is inevitable and must be accommodated within certain negotiated limits,' he says, adding that 'Russia, in my view, is misunderstood, has been badly handled by the West over the last twenty years and some double standards are being applied.' This type of strategic judgement, implicitly devolving authority to these two big emerging powers, might be termed by its adherents as realpolitik and its critics as appeasement.

Furthermore, the calculation that Russia or even Syria must be 'brought on-side' comes more easily in Europe than in the United States, where the adherence to certain revolutionary and democratic ideals is central to the national discourse. However, the failure of either intervention in Iraq or the Arab Spring to produce meaningful democratic change in the Middle East has caused a type of policy paralysis in Washington. Try to find people to answer the question 'Should the US still advocate the spread of democracy in the Arab world?' as we on *Newsnight* recently did, and you will find precious few think-tankers or former officials willing to engage.

In the UK and other European countries, having cut their military faster and deeper than the US post-Cold War, the loss of options resulting from the multi-polar world is even more obvious. Having explicitly acknowledged years ago that it could only wage war against another state as part of a US-led or Nato coalition, and since it is plainly impossible for the country to align with a new player like Russia or China, Britain's 'strategic choices' have become limited to whether to join in some new US-led adventure or not.

For David Cameron's Conservatives at the time of the 2010 election, the answer to questions about the conduct of foreign policy in an age of austerity and war weariness was that there should be more of a hardheaded evaluation of national interest in joining future international coalitions and, implicitly, a greater reluctance to weigh in on others' fights. However, the coalition led by Mr Cameron has played a leading role in the strikes on Libya in 2011, advocated hitting President Assad's regime in Syria (but failed to get parliamentary agreement to do so), and joined air action against Islamic State militants in 2014. As Middle Eastern countries have fallen into chaos (helped in some cases on the road to ruin by the West, and in others managing it all on their own) this military action has started to resemble firefighting or crisis management rather than a grand design for the region. Indeed, when such attacks follow the murder of hostages it starts to look a little like a modern form of gunboat diplomacy.

But of course these days 'the natives' can sometimes hit back hard. The development of sophisticated military capabilities by many countries, and indeed even non-state groups, as al-Qaeda showed on 9/11, can harm Western societies in a way that would have been unimaginable 150 years ago, during the time of Victorian punitive operations. The question now for Western policy-makers is about the political or diplomatic implications of the new alliances they will need in order to preserve their interests or to intervene in ungoverned space. It is quite possible that noisy populations, animated by nationalism, will find it so hard to cooperate on a consistent basis that each new challenge will have to be met by some new, and perhaps improbable, coalition of the willing. Thus Iran in 2014 has helped the US in its goal of trying to prop up the new Iraqi government even though the US insists that it is still working for the overthrow of the Assad government in Syria, an Iranian ally. Is this the reality of a true multi-polar world? Or is this outcome actually worse and even more diffuse than multi-polarity, which many foreign policy practitioners would assume involved a handful of leading states – poly-polarity, perhaps?

We cannot even assume 'the West' will remain a cohesive bloc under the stress of austerity and rival nationalisms. Britain might exit the EU or a further crisis with Russia cause the fragmentation of Nato. The rise of extreme nationalist movements in France, Greece and Hungary could also endanger the future of the EU; even if the challenge did not grow that serious, it might still threaten the coherence of its response to external challenges.

It may be, on the contrary, that out of these increasingly unlikely combinations comes a move towards a new kind of bi-polarity, with economics as its driver. In this future, the United States would continue to ally itself with Europe, the Gulf States and India. China and Russia would form a rival bloc, based around an alternative to the old dollar-based global economic model. 'We already see that more and more countries are looking for ways to become less dependent on the dollar and are setting up alternative financial and payments systems and reserve currencies,' President Putin told the Valdai Club in 2014, arguing that, in their use of sanctions or globalisation to promote their own national interests, 'I think that our American friends are quite simply cutting the branch they are sitting on.'

If these trends produce a new trading bloc and de facto alliance, Russia's large nuclear arsenal and advanced defence industry would be key assets. However, some detect, in the terms the Kremlin has conceded on a huge new gas deal or the Siberian mineral concessions it is giving to its eastern partner, signs that China would effectively subsume its Russian partner under such an arrangement. The Chinese, meanwhile, are seeking to further their reach and make new allies, not only with growing investment in Africa but also with military engagements such as joint exercises with the Iranian navy in October 2014. It is easy to see how Iran, North Korea and even Pakistan might gravitate towards this new power group.

The counter to this idea is that a global preference for the dollar and even the euro will prevent Russia and China from establishing a new trading bloc in tandem with a more potent strategic alliance. But while many senior military people I've spoken to, including General Sir Peter Wall, believe that economic pressure will continue to provide a key lever to counteract 'hybrid' or deniable warfare of the kind practised by President Putin in Ukraine, they also believe that a forthright Nato deterrent response is required. 'We need to be prepared to draw lines and challenge Russian adventurism,' he asserts, reflecting that 'the Cold War taught us that de-escalating against the Russians has its limitations, even though it may be attractive in the short term.'

Whether we see a new binary division in the world, a new Cold War or more of a multi-polar set-up, the odds of getting consensus on global challenges become longer. That undermines the chances of agreement on everything from climate change to how a pariah state is handled. In such a future international dystopia, problems will escalate faster and potentially to more devastating effect. More actors – state and otherwise – will be in possession of more advanced weapons including, as time passes, nuclear, chemical and biological arms. As consensus breaks down and the global power balance shifts, so deterrence, including even its nuclear variety, could easily falter too.

In 2001 al-Qaeda attacked the United States. It was not deterred, perhaps because it underestimated the consequences for its own security or anticipated a global Muslim response that did not quite materialise. In 2014, an airliner was shot down over eastern Ukraine, with some adverse results for Russia but without derailing the progress of Moscow's client militias towards secession from Ukraine. Exactly who brought down that aircraft and whether it was simply a terrible mistake matter less in this context than the fact that warring parties can now act in this way with apparent impunity.

Today many Western countries are incapable of defending themselves even from the type of threats that a group like al-Qaeda might mount. Early in 2014 an Ethiopian Airlines plane was hijacked and flew into Swiss airspace unescorted, landing at Geneva airport. Subsequent enquiries established that the Swiss air force had failed to scramble because the incident happened at a weekend, and fighter cover had become limited to office hours on weekdays. Some other

European countries would have fared no better, and could equally do little to prevent a complex sea-borne terrorist attack on the Mumbai pattern, or a merchant vessel being used against them as a floating bomb. Even countries like Spain and Germany now have sufficiently thin air cover as to make a 9/11-type attack possible at certain times.

When it comes to the more sophisticated threat from state armed forces, the limits are even more glaring. Scandinavian and Baltic countries have recently found Russian incursions into their air and sea space increasing as a result of new East–West tensions. Sufficiently alarmed by the poor readiness of their small armed forces, Norway, Sweden and Finland are all now looking at speeding up new fighter purchases. Baltic states, meanwhile, have appealed for and received Nato help.

What if the pessimists about Russian intentions are right and the Western alliance soon finds itself tested in those Baltic republics? How would the British public react to a day in which twenty of their soldiers, hurriedly sent over in support of a Nato ally, had been killed by Russian separatists? Or what if a flare-up of tensions on the Korean peninsula caused a Japanese or an American ship to be sunk 'by accident'? Is there the political will to respond militarily, even assuming the capability is adequate? In Washington and other Western capitals the assumption for some years now has been that economic sanctions are often the best form of response to such a challenge. But if the recent trend by some countries to sidestep the West and develop their own economic ties continues, then this form of deterrence will again be weakened. Against enemies like ISIS, leverage is even weaker. How would Western countries react if the militants seemed poised to overthrow a major Gulf monarchy?

When considering the way the West might handle a future crisis with Russia – say over one of the Baltic states – not everyone is confident that they would stand up for the country that had been picked upon, and invoke the principle of common defence contained in Article 5 of the Nato treaty. Could the US be relied upon in such circumstances? General Sir Richard Shirreff, formerly the alliance's second-ranking officer, says yes, but astoundingly questions the UK's commitment: 'I'm much more concerned that the House of Commons would prevent the British government from honouring its Article 5 commitment under collective defence.' If he is right, and the issue is one of political weakness, then even greater military capability might be of little use.

As these security challenges emerge, divergent perceptions create their own risks of misperception. When I asked Nato's Secretary General, Jens Stoltenberg, in a BBC interview whether there was a new Cold War, he replied very directly, 'No.' President Obama has said the same thing. Yet Russian analysts, even those like the former Soviet colonel Dmitri Trenin, who now runs the Carnegie Endowment for International Peace's Moscow think tank, see things very differently. 'I think that the conflict that we've entered into, and it is a conflict and a major one between Russia on the one hand and the West on the other hand, is about bigger things than Ukraine,' he told me, adding ominously when asked the same question that I'd posed to Jens Stoltenberg, 'It may not necessarily be a Cold War that we may be facing, unless we're very careful. It may be a hot war.'

Are Western countries being complacent, failing to

tell their people about the potential gravity of this new threat to European security? The leaders of some northern countries such as Poland and Finland have stated things very plainly and set about increasing military preparedness. But these nations, sharing historical memories of being subject peoples of the Russian empire, are hardly typical. When I asked one of Britain's service chiefs whether he thought the government was taking the new threat seriously, he replied, 'They are too terrified of the public spending implications of saying so, and increasing defence at the expense of other sectors.'

'I don't think there's been the political turnaround yet,' says Francis Fukuyama, who believes that democratic leaders are not yet grasping the implications of change in Russia. 'I think, unfortunately, that begins in the United States, where I think President Obama has been exclusively focused on terrorism in the Middle East and ... he's not actually preparing the country for the fact that there's this longer-term struggle in Europe,' he told me in an interview, and 'European politicians are very reluctant too, for economic reasons.'

Politically disunited, prosperous and practically undefended, Europe starts to look distinctly vulnerable. While its own citizens dwell on the effects of prolonged recession, millions of others, seeking to escape the turmoil of Africa or the Middle East, are already trying to have some of that prosperity – by boarding a leaky ship in Libya or being hidden in a Turkish truck. Non-state groups, from pirates to kidnappers or organised crime syndicates, are making more aggressive attempts to skim Europe's wealth. As for state-on-state conflict, many European leaders might hope it has been consigned to the past, but the large-scale theft of intellectual property and cyber espionage practised by China, Russia and Iran suggest a deliberate policy by national governments.

Few people five years ago would have predicted the dismemberment of Ukraine; that Iran and the US would end up on the same side in Iraq; or that big slices of Middle Eastern airspace would be deemed unsafe for air travel. There's little point, then, in me spilling too much ink with hypotheticals. Clearly, there could be all manner of positive global developments. Equally, things could get even worse. Vladimir

Putin could be replaced by someone of even stronger nationalist tendencies, or China could calculate that it was no longer in its interests to finance the US deficit. Militancy could triumph in Pakistan, and its leaders gain control of nuclear weapons. While the Islamic State offensive in Iraq and Syria has lost some momentum since the start of the American-led strikes, it could still become a major threat to global security if, for example, it threatened to engulf Lebanon, Jordan or even Saudi Arabia. Lieutenant-General Sir Graeme Lamb, deputy commander of the coalition forces in Iraq in 2006–7, believes such a scenario would 'open the gates of hell – it would be end of days stuff'.

In London, Washington and Berlin there is a consensus that the international security environment is deteriorating, yet beyond speechifying, there appears to be little will to anything about it. Nato leaders meet at summits and agree that they should aim to spend 2 per cent of their GDP on defence – in ten years' time. Some, like Angela Merkel, then fly home and continue to push through cuts that take them well below that target. Others, such as David Cameron, proudly said they have met the 2 per cent target (in 2014), but batted away well-reasoned academic analyses that suggest maintaining this spending level will require significant cash increases in coming years, saying they don't accept the figures.

Likewise, these leaders, if you take their public statements at face value, agree that Russia's recent actions have broken the rules established to keep the peace not just since the fall of the USSR, but since 1945. Some have used comparisons with the 1930s. Surely, then, this type of reflection should cause them to revisit cuts made at the end of the Cold War that assumed the military threat to Western Europe had disappeared.

There is some rethinking going on, to be sure. At the end of the Nato Wales summit in 2014, Anders Fogh Rasmussen, the outgoing Secretary General, said that the pledge to spend 2 per cent of GDP 'marks a turning point'. America is slowing its cuts. Some European countries are now looking again at basic issues of self-defence such as fighter or maritime cover.

Overall, though, there has been no meaningful reassessment of national priorities in the Western alliance's biggest countries, despite the comparisons of Russia's current behaviour with the 1930s, or the disintegration of some Middle East states. When given some leeway by tough fiscal management, additional money is available, on the evidence of the UK prime minister's 2014 speech to the party conference. However, it is used not to whittle down the deficit faster, or to restore some capability to the military or other public services, but for promises of tax cuts.

It's questionable whether even a sudden rearmament drive could turn the West's military decline around quickly. The sums involved would be colossal, the lead times required for modern weapons development are long, and the system of military procurement has for too long been geared to the interests of contractors rather than making war-winning equipment. And underlying it all is the hard reality of Western economic stagnation, while geopolitical rivals from China, to India, to Brazil power ahead.

The size of Western armed forces, their stocks of weaponry and their readiness for combat all continue to decline by most indices. The Edge, the West's advantage, and along with it that ability to deter people in parts of the world from doing desperate things, is going, if it has not already disappeared. If events in

Ukraine or the Middle East have not already made this clear, some other crisis will soon be along to do so.

The US and its Nato allies will find it increasingly difficult to protect their interests or to act for the broader good, as they did in reversing Saddam Hussein's aggression against Kuwait in 1991 or in containing the Yugoslav wars a few years later. Instead they will more often find themselves watching from the sidelines as ungoverned space expands and the values prized in liberal democracies are violated. How far China, Russia or other regional powers will go to fill this vacuum, or to throw their weight around, we don't yet know. Common approaches to major security challenges are however likely to prove more elusive than ever.

One aspect of the Western response to crises – from Syria to Sudan – remains vibrant: words. We can expect more of those; carefully worded presidential or prime ministerial statements in response to coups, massacres and invasions. But we should be in no doubt that the ability and willingness to act have declined markedly, and are set to do so further.

Notes

Chapter 1: The Tides of Power

8 *So Germany has also wielded the axe*: 'Nato's Military Decline', *Wall Street Journal*, 25 March 2014.

10 *further cuts to military spending*: *The Military Balance 2014: The Annual Assessment of Global Military Capabilities and Defence Economics* (London: International Institute for Strategic Studies, 2014).

11 *Footing three-quarters of the Nato bill*: 'Nato's Military Decline'.

12 *In 2014, the United States Air Force*: Ibid.

13 *'European countries have effectively disarmed themselves'*: General Sir Richard Shirreff, interview with the author, 2014.

Chapter 2: Force Multipliers

27 *'clubbed like baby seals'*: 'F35 fighter would be clubbed like baby seals in combat', Nextbigfuture, 14 August 2013, <http://nextbigfuture.com/2013/08/f35-fighter-would-be-clubbed-like-baby.html>.

38 *recently announced the intention to spend:* 'Report: Saudi Arabia Eyes Buying German Submarines', Defense News, 3 November 2013, citing an original report in Germany's *Bild am Sonntag* newspaper.

Chapter 3: Kneel or Starve

42 *provided some substance to the reports*: Zack Baddorf, 'Syria Is Obama's Rwanda', Vice News, 3 June 2014, <https://news.vice.com/article/syria-is-obamas-rwanda>.

44 *'a creeping aversion to risk ...'*: General Sir Nick Houghton, Annual Chief of the Defence Staff Lecture, Royal United Services Institute, 18 December 2013. Transcript available at <https://www.rusi.org/events/past/ref:E5284A3D06EFFD>.

44–5 *'War weariness or maybe better termed "war wariness" ...'*: General Stan McChrystal, correspondence with the author.

48 *'post-heroic warfare'*: Edward N. Luttwak, 'Toward Post-Heroic Warfare', *Foreign Affairs*, May/June 1995.

49 *One excellent example of this mentality:* Author conversations with Generals Jackson and Clark. Jackson also

re-told the story in *Soldier: The Autobiography* (London: Bantam, 2008).

52–3 *'I'm sceptical of the war-weariness theory . . .'*: General Sir Richard Shirreff, correspondence with the author, 2014.

53 *'As a percentage of people, the number involved . . .'*: Admiral Bill Fallon, interview with the author, 2014.

54–5 *'There is a prejudice against decisive military engagement . . .'*: General Sir Peter Wall, correspondence with the author, 2014.

60 *'the next fifteen to twenty years . . .'*: Burrows, *The Future, Declassified.*

Chapter 4: The Faltering Giant

67 *In 2012 Robert Kagan wrote persuasively*: Robert Kagan, 'Not Fade Away: The Myth of American Decline', *New Republic*, 11 January 2012.

68 *'the coming catastrophe is always coming . . .'*: Adam Gopnik, 'Decline, Fall, Rinse, Repeat: Is America Going Down?', *New Yorker*, 12 September 2011.

69 *'the most fundamental threat to the US . . .'*: General Stan McChrystal, correspondence with the author, 2014.

69 *'Our biggest problem,'*: Admiral Bill Fallon, interview with the author, 2014.

77–8 *'Russia and China don't report their actual defense spending . . .'*: Mitt Romney, 'The need for a mighty US military', *Washington Post*, 4 September 2014.

78–9 *'If the US is unwilling or less able . . .'*: Burrows, *The Future, Declassified.*

79 *'in the US Navy the level of readiness . . .'*: Admiral Bill
    Fallon, interview with the author, 2014.

Chapter 5: The Multi-Polar World

85 *'In a more volatile geopolitical situation,'*: Quoted in Paul
    Goble, 'Putin Believes He Can Win a War with
    NATO, Piontkovsky Says', The Interpreter, 10 August
    2014,   <http://www.interpretermag.com/putin-
    believes-he-can-win-a-war-with-nato-piontkovsky-sa
    ys/>.

87 *'if we ever had to go into that and fight . . .'*: General Philip
    Breedlove, Department of Defense Press Briefing,
    Pentagon Briefing Room, 16 September 2014.
    Transcript available at <http://www.defense.gov/
    Transcripts/Transcript.aspx?TranscriptID=5503>.

92–3 *'There's been pretty much unrestricted Chinese aggression . . .'*:
    Admiral Bill Fallon, interview with the author, 2014.

93 *'a new model of great power relations'*: See Cheng Li inter-
    view, 'A New Type of Major Power Relationship?',
    Georgetown Journal of International Affairs, 26
    September 2014, <http://www.brookings.edu/
    research/interviews/2014/09/26-new-type-power-
    relationship-li>.

93 *'busy trying to define a new great power relationship'*: John
    Kerry, US Vision for Asia-Pacific Engagement:
    Remarks, East-West Center, Honolulu, 13 August
    2014. Transcript available at <http://www.state.gov/
    secretary/remarks/2014/08/230597.htm>.

93 *'it is a foregone conclusion ...'*: Burrows, *The Future, Declassified.*

94 *'The biggest issue for the US long term ...'*: Admiral Bill Fallon, interview with the author, 2014.

96 *'I believe that extreme non-state organisations like ISIS ...'*: Lord Richards, correspondence with the author, 2015.

97–8 *In 2014, the International Institute for Strategic Studies assessed*: *The Military Balance 2014: The Annual Assessment of Global Military Capabilities and Defence Economics* (London: International Institute for Strategic Studies, 2014).

Chapter 6: The Vanishing Consensus

106 *the 'end of history'*: See Francis Fukuyama, 'The End of History?', *National Interest*, 1989.

109 *An article by Zhou Xiaoping*: Amy Quin, 'Undermining China, One Knockout at a Time', *New York Times* Sinosphere blog, 17 July 2014, <http://sinosphere. blogs.nytimes.com/2014/07/17/undermining-china-one-knockout-at-a-time/?_r=0>.

110 *'They actually want to present Russia as a baddie and a bully,'*: Quoted in Bridget Kendall, 'Hybrid warfare: The new conflict between East and West', BBC News website, 6 November 2014, <http://www.bbc.co.uk/news/world-europe-29903395>.

111 *'for now, we can't identify shared values with Russia ...'*: Sir John Sawers, 'The Limits of Security', War Studies 2015 Annual Lecture, Department of War Studies,

King's College London, 16 February 2015. Transcript available at <http://www.kcl.ac.uk/sspp/depart-ments/warstudies/news/newsrecords/sawers.aspx>.

112 *'Russia's actions in Ukraine challenge [the] post-war order.'*: Remarks by President Obama in Address to the United Nations General Assembly, 24 September 2014. Transcript available at <http://www.whitehouse.gov/the-press-office/2014/09/24/remarks-president-obama-address-united-nations-general-assembly>.

112 *'I think we're in a period of prolonged societal conflict ...'*: James Kitfield, 'Flynn's Last Interview: Iconoclast Departs DIA With A Warning', Breaking Defense, 7 August 2014, <http://breakingdefense.com/2014/08/flynns-last-interview-intel-iconoclast-departs-dia-with-a-warning/>.

114 *The cumulative effects of American cuts and others' increases*: *The Military Balance 2015*.

114 *'Putin knows that the West cannot cross the red line ...'*: Mikhail Shishkin, 'Russia, Ukraine and Europe have been into Vladimir Putin's black hole of fear', *Guardian*, 18 September 2014.

116 *'attempts at restoring the mono-polar world'*: Sergey Lavrov, remarks accessed via @mfa_russia Twitter account.

Chapter 7: Back to the Jungle

122 *'The business of multi-polarity is very real now,'*: Admiral Bill Fallon, interview with the author, 2014.

124 *'I think that this formula accurately describes ...'*: Vladimir

Putin, Meeting of the Valdai International Discussion Club, 24 October 2014. Excerpts from the transcript available at <http://www.rusemb.org.uk/foreignpolicy/2659>.

125 *'In the near term,'*: General Stan McChrystal, correspondence with the author, 2014.

125 *'It will do if we remain as detached . . .'*: General Sir Peter Wall, correspondence with the author, 2014.

127 *'government of the people and by the people . . .'*: Remarks by the President on a New Beginning, Cairo University, 4 June 2009. Transcript available at <http://www.whitehouse.gov/the-press-office/ remarks-president-cairo-university-6-04-09>.

128–9 *'China's rise is inevitable . . .'*: Lord Richards, correspondence with the author, 2014.

133 *'I think that our American friends . . .'*: Vladimir Putin, Meeting of the Valdai International Discussion Club, op. cit.

134 *'We need to be prepared to draw lines . . .'*: General Sir Peter Wall, correspondence with the author, 2014.

137–8 *'I'm much more concerned that . . .'*: General Sir Richard Shirreff, correspondence with the author, 2014.

139 *'I don't think there's been the political turnaround yet,'*: Francis Fukuyama, interview with the author, 2014.

141 *'open the gates of hell . . .'*: Lieutenant-General Sir Graeme Lamb, interview with the author, 2014.

Suggested Reading

Bobbitt, Philip, *The Shield of Achilles: War, Peace and the Course of History* (London: Allen Lane, 2002)

Burrows, Mathew, *The Future, Declassified: Megatrends That Will Undo the World Unless We Take Action* (New York: Palgrave Macmillan, 2014)

Coker, Christopher, *The Improbable War: China, the United States and the Logic of Great Power Conflict* (London: C. Hurst & Co., 2015)

Elliott, Christopher L., *High Command: British Military Leadership in the Iraq and Afghanistan Wars* (London: C. Hurst & Co., 2015)

Fairweather, Jack, *A War of Choice: The British in Iraq 2003–9* (London: Jonathan Cape, 2011)

Freedman, Lawrence, *Strategy: A History* (New York: Oxford University Press, 2013)

Kennedy, Paul, *The Rise and Fall of the Great Powers: Economic Change and Military Conflict from 1500–2000* (London: Fontana Press, 1989)

The Military Balance 2015: The Annual Assessment of Global Military Capabilities and Defence Economics (London: International Institute for Strategic Studies, 2015)

Morris, Ian, *War, What is it Good For?: The Role of Conflict in Civilisation, from Primates to Robots* (London: Profile Books, 2014)

Richards, General David, *Taking Command* (London: Headline, 2014)

Ricks, Thomas E., *The Gamble: General Petraeus and the Untold Story of the American Surge in Iraq, 2006–2008* (London: Allen Lane, 2009)

Simpson, Emile, *War From the Ground Up: Twenty-First-Century Combat as Politics* (London: C. Hurst & Co., 2012)

Van Creveld, Martin, *The Transformation of War* (1991; London: Simon and Schuster, 2009)

Woodward, Bob, *Obama's Wars* (London: Simon and Schuster, 2010)

Acknowledgements

This book started life before the Russian annexation of Crimea, the war in east Ukraine, and the capture of Mosul by ISIS. I am all the more grateful therefore for Tim Whiting at Little, Brown for seeing the point of it and commissioning *The Edge* way back then. I am grateful too to Zoe Gullen and David Bamford at the publishers for getting the manuscript into shape, amid a barrage of constant adjustments from me.

Jonathan Lloyd, my agent, did the deal with his usual panache. My wife Hilary and children also deserve thanks for putting up with the usual writer's introspection and hours spent in the study.

Index